The Promise at the
Dairy Queen

The Promise at the Dairy Queen

A Tale of a Marriage and Motherhood

DOROTHY SINCLAIR

THE PROMISE AT THE DAIRY QUEEN
A TALE OF A MARRIAGE AND MOTHERHOOD

iUniverse books may be ordered through booksellers or by contacting:

iUniverse
1663 Liberty Drive
Bloomington, IN 47403
www.iuniverse.com
1-800-Authors (1-800-288-4677)

Because of the dynamic nature of the Internet, any web addresses or links contained in this book may have changed since publication and may no longer be valid. The views expressed in this work are solely those of the author and do not necessarily reflect the views of the publisher, and the publisher hereby disclaims any responsibility for them.

Any people depicted in stock imagery provided by Thinkstock are models, and such images are being used for illustrative purposes only.
Certain stock imagery © Thinkstock.

ISBN: 978-1-4917-8571-3 (sc)
ISBN: 978-1-4917-8572-0 (e)

Library of Congress Control Number: 2015921122

Print information available on the last page.

iUniverse rev. date: 12/28/2015

Karl & Dorothy in Greece, 1965

ACKNOWLEDGEMENTS

Thanks to my inimitable teacher and mentor, playwright Donald Freed, to his incredible helpmate Patty-Rae, and to all the members of his Writers Workshop for keeping me continually smiling and writing. Thanks to my family who encouraged me in this venture. A special thank-you to my granddaughters, Zoe and Keeley, for their tireless interest in family photos, without which this project might never have seen the light of day.

INTRODUCTION

I find myself deep into a century in which I am not yet totally comfortable, neither with the technology nor the customs, which change with the speed of light. The wedding about which I write took place during what came to be known as "The McCarthy Era"– smack in the middle of the nineteen hundreds. This put me always on the cusp, like a tight-rope walker constantly performing a balancing act. Divorce, so commonplace today, was rare in those days whereas the words *'til death do us part* have now all but lost their meaning.

My earlier memoir, *You Can Take the Girl Out of Chicago*, proved that I was much ahead of my time, yet still enough of a romantic to be shocked and inconsolable when my marriage fell apart. The names Betty Friedan and Gloria Steinem were not yet part of my lexicon, the feminist movement was nearly a decade into the future. Not feeling entitled to "have it all" played havoc with my relationship to the man with whom I had intended to spend the rest of my life. My husband Karl was the father of my two children. As such, he has remained a part of my life that only he could fulfill. I have attempted to paint an accurate but lighthearted picture of him and of those years we spent together.

CONTENTS

PART ONE:

CHICAGO

MATCH DOT COM,
CIRCA 1949

My year and a half of playing "struggling actress" in New York City proved both a happy and a painful experience. Although I had met (i.e. had affairs with) poets and playwrights and musicians of renown by working in The Four Seasons Book Shop in Greenwich Village, I had failed in my attempts to find an affordable apartment or to get a role on Broadway. When I arrived back in Chicago with my tail between my legs, my distraught father offered to finance some much needed therapy.

As my psychoanalysis approached its third year my analyst, Dr. Greene, appeared to be losing patience. "What are you going to find wrong with *this* one?" He would question as I rejected man after man. Chicago seemed sorely lacking in what I called *appropriate* suitors. Too insecure, too unattractive, too dull, too broke. I whined about a young woman I had met at a political rally who had become my friend. "Bernice is smart and nice, but her figure isn't nearly as good as mine. She's got a pretty face, but she's kind of chubby. So how come she's got Karl *and* Jake, two guys she's serious about?" Secretly I consoled myself with the thought that neither of them could be too attractive. How wrong was I!

Bernice invited me to attend a party with her at a grand old craftsman mansion in the Hyde Park neighborhood. (The same neighborhood that decades later would produce the 44th president of the United States.) Since both of her boyfriends were to attend I went eagerly, knowing I'd get a first hand look. The party was in full swing. A guitar player strummed to the lyrics of *It's Better With a Union Maid* as we sipped red wine from paper cups under an oak staircase. Bernice pointed across the room: "There's Jake. Over there. Talking to that tall black guy." A cute redhead, Jake was a doll.

Nearing thirty and anxious to start a family, Bernice reached a decision. She felt Jake was better marriage material than Karl and that they could have a happy life together. She would break up with Karl. My curiosity peaked. Surely this Karl couldn't be so great if she intended to toss him over. I wondered if he was going to show. It had begun to rain. The party was winding down when an attractive 5'10" guy in classic tan trench coat and floppy felt hat dashed in and headed straight for the wine. No way could this be Karl. I already knew that he was in his last year of med school and here he was—just my type! Bernice is really, truly dumping this guy? *Not good marriage material?* I could only wonder why. Why?

Introductions were made and we bantered a little before he had to rush home to study. It wouldn't have taken a Richter Scale to register the chemistry. The next day Bernice phoned to tell me that he had asked if it was OK with her if he called me and would she give him my phone number and she wanted to know if that was OK with me. OK? *OK?* She had to be kidding!

MIAMI DETOUR

We were propped up together on his narrow bed, sipping bourbon, smoking a well-deserved cigarette. I should have been in heaven. But I was troubled. I was in the midst of a huge dilemma. My timing was way off. If it were just me I could have unpacked my bags and canceled my flight. But it was not just me. I could hear my mother: "What do you mean you're not going? Make up your mind once and for all. You're driving us crazy!"

Finally I had had a date with the most wonderful man I had met since the night years before in the St. Louis Airport, when I first glimpsed Jay Landesman leaning against his woody station wagon. Karl had driven to Rush Street in his old Willys *(what is it with me and vintage cars?)* "I hope you like jazz." More statement than question, it required no answer. How could I *not* like jazz? Inside the murky *Blue Note Club* the owner, Ruth Reinhart, greeted him like an old friend, "Welcome, welcome. Best table for two." Flashing me a warm smile she seated us just close enough to the bandstand. Karl took my hand in his, drumming on the table in perfect time with the music. I made no move to resist. My hand inside his felt like a perfect fit–exciting yet safe. Bill Reinhart put down his clarinet and took the mike. A skinny balding white guy, he perfectly mimicked the guttural tone of a New Orleans native: *I know why I waited. Know why I've been blue. It's to be with someone, Exactly like you.* Shock waves. Magic. The evening was perfect. We ended it on the narrow bed in his cold water flat on the Near North Side—a short distance from Navy Pier, where he was in his last year at Illinois Medical School.

In the morning I was treated to a lukewarm shower in a stall he had rigged in the middle of his kitchen. We shared coffee and toast, courtesy of an oven that obliged us by springing to life after the third match. He told me of his plans to begin his internship in Brooklyn following graduation in June. He told me of serving in India during World War II, of his life as a labor organizer–the reason his medical studies began so late and why he is a decade older than many of his classmates. Could this be the guy I have been waiting for? The "yes" columns were totaling up. *Dr. Right* was flashing all over him.

While he showered I was free to inspect his tiny apartment. Books everywhere. An old fashioned fireplace with a mantel above it, on which rests a picture of a smiling little boy who looks to be about five. Uh, oh–a potential deal breaker. I want no involvement with a guy with baggage. He assured me that this is Arthur, his adorable young nephew. True, he had a brief marriage while in the army but no, no, he has no children, although he would like to one day.

We parted reluctantly—he to his classes, me to my parents' house where the rehearsed lie about last night's whereabouts is already on my lips. That we will meet that evening, and probably the next, is almost a given. I was unable to permit myself to luxuriate in the happiness I felt in my bones. Even though life in Chicago had become more interesting since I had become a member of an *agit-prop* acting company called Stage for Action, living at home with my parents was driving me crazy. I had to get away. Miami was on my radar thanks to my old college chum, Thalia.

Thalia had arrived in my junior year at Madison as a freshman from Florida, an eager buxom beauty with a bit of a drawl. Since she was a year younger than I, this became my first opportunity to adopt the role of a mentor. Half way into her first semester, Thalia slipped on the ice at the top of the hill on which sits the University of Wisconsin, landing her with a broken leg and a pair of crutches. Poor Thal! A bad break in more ways than one. She was one of the best jitter-buggers on campus, often winning contests with my talented boyfriend, Stan Moldawsky. I assumed she would have to withdraw for the remainder of the year, wasting all the work she had so far accomplished. That was the scenario most coeds would have followed. But most coeds didn't have a mother like Doris.

Doris Yaffey had worked hard to get her somewhat flighty eldest daughter into college, and she had no intention of giving up now. Before the week was out, she was on a plane for Madison. She moved into Thalia's room in our dorm explaining her plan of action during our first dinner together. Beginning Monday morning, she would attend every one of her daughter's classes, receive the assignments, and relay everything. Thalia would be off crutches before finals and with her mother's help, pass with flying colors.

Thalia had definitely inherited her looks from her maternal side. Doris was a beauty, a lively, talkative woman whose demeanor belied her years. Even so, this was a time when people over thirty other than professors were rarely seen on campus, much less taking notes at a classroom desk. I rained on her parade: "It'll never work. They'll never let you do it and even if they would, how could you possibly teach Thalia everything?"

"Darahthee" Doris insisted, in her own version of my name, "The word *never* is not in my vocabulary. I'm going to do this for Thal and it will all work out. It's got to. We've sacrificed financially to get her here. I've left my husband alone for months. You'll see. Everything will be O.K."

For the next several weeks we became accustomed to the sight of an older woman trudging up the hill, notebooks in hand. Though she was enthusiastic about all of Thalia's classes, her main focus soon became a cutting edge topic known as *Semantics*. Wisconsin University had scored a coup with the inclusion on its faculty of the leading figure in the field, the charismatic S.I. Hayakawa. Dr. Hayakawa believed in the supreme importance of words; the choice of language is reflective of all our thinking, conscious as well as subconscious. Doris was spellbound–she really "got it." Next she began challenging every word that escaped our lips, stopping everyone mid-sentence, digging, digging, digging into our motivations. "What did you mean by that? Why did you use that phrase?" Holding a normal conversation with her became impossible. Proselytizing is almost always annoying, but Doris could beat out any religious zealot. In between long telephone conversations with her husband Marv, were her rambling letters. When Marv dismissed these as merely the latest in a series of his wife's passing fads, she threatened to divorce him. And she meant it. He'd better get aboard her bandwagon, *or else*. Doris did get Thalia through her finals, but by the time she left Madison we all agreed she had become a royal pain. And now here I am, five years later, willingly subjecting myself to a double dose of Doris.

If it was only me. But it wasn't. Adding to my ambivalence there was also my beloved Aunt Flo to consider. "How can you leave me for such a long time?" she challenged as we shopped for bras in Marshall Field's. "If this guy is as great as you think, don't take a chance by going out of town!" Flo's advice usually proved to be wise.

Time for a return visit to my guru, my analyst Dr. Greene.

"What's the crisis, Dee? I thought we had terminated therapy while you moved down to Miami."

"I know, I know I already said good-bye when you told me it was O.K. to take the job. But now things have changed. What do I do?"

I was aware that this was an inappropriate question, violating all the rules of good Freudian analysis. "Tell me what to do" would inevitably be followed by "What do *you* think you should do?" However, I felt by this time I had earned the right. Dr. Greene bent the rules. And handed me a surprise.

"Dee, once again you resorted to your old pattern of rushing into sex too soon. Karl really hasn't had a chance to know who you are. How do you suppose he'll view you if he sees you as someone with no integrity, someone who could flippantly violate a commitment and leave others in the lurch? If he's serious about you, he will wait for you. He might even follow you down there, if only for a few days. No, no, you must behave like a grown up, not a flighty, impulsive girl. Your bags are packed. Ship them to Miami."

Here was the Big Daddy who had invested hours in trying to help his patient find an appropriate Jewish husband. Now he was advising me to take a risk. However, he has given me a scenario. I must not leave town until I have extracted a promise from Karl to join me in Florida for a weekend. I'll try to lure him with the promise of fun filled days alternating between surf, sand, and sex. I'll agonize over my impending departure, proving what a dependable, reliable person I am by fulfilling a commitment. Good marriage material.

Thalia had left Wisconsin to complete her education at a local Miami college and moved back in with her parents. An accomplished pianist, she capitalized on her talent by teaching music to three and four year-olds. She had an excellent job at the Hebrew Academy Nursery School where parents, faculty and students alike, adored her. Within those walls she could do no wrong. When she recommended her friend from Chicago as someone qualified to teach Creative Dramatics, the school principal hired me with little more than a telephone interview.

There was one other reason for my hasty acceptance. In Miami, my winsome friend found herself caught up in a whirlwind of dates that she could barely handle. World War II had just ended. In addition to many 4-F's (those with medical discharges) who had stayed behind, the city was loaded with returning servicemen anxious to marry and settle down. By now Thalia was romantically involved with a handsome young dentist just starting out in practice. Though he was smitten, Thal, reluctant to break hearts, continued with her dating game. She really could use someone to handle the surplus. Doris was thoroughly convinced that young Phillip was the perfect catch for Thalia and eager that she discourage other suitors before something went awry. Here's where I came into the picture. The plan was for me to work beside my pal in the a.m. and handle some of her leftovers in the evening. There was Ted, a successful, pudgy plastic surgeon. Ted might or might not be gay, but he had lots of money, was extremely generous, and eager to squire an attractive young woman about town. There was Jack, a bearded almost-intellectual, who owned a small but prestigious bookstore on Lincoln Road. More my speed. Then there was Arnie, the Jewish accountant, a nerdy-looking sweet four-eyes, on the hunt for a permanent relationship. And that was just the start. There were plenty others around that I could captivate on my own. The single men in this resort city shared one caveat: their date must not be a tourist but rather a permanent resident.

None of them cared to waste emotion or money on someone who might leave town on a moment's notice. Thalia had already committed me to a charming one-bedroom apartment on Indian Creek Avenue. Perfect! A job, and an apartment, certainly qualified me as someone who was settling "permanently" in Miami Beach.

Doris was ecstatic. She took me aside at once with instructions. "Dahr-a-thee, Philip is crazy about Thal and he's ready to propose. But I'm afraid she'll lose him if she doesn't give him her undivided attention. If you could spend time with those other guys it would be terrific. The only thing is, I don't want you to distract her, so please don't try to double date with her or see too much of her. Just allow her to concentrate on Phillip."

O.K. Doris, whatever you say, but this is going to be a bit frustrating because I had hoped to spend more time with my delightful friend. I couldn't risk Doris's wrath. Thalia and I saw each other mornings at work and that was about it. The plan to palm me off on Ted and Jack and Arnie worked like a charm. For the first time in my life I had to keep a calendar so as not to lose track of my dates. Dances and dinners with Ted and the local medical community on Saturdays, picnics and family dinners with Arnie, autograph parties at his shop with Jack, pastrami sandwiches with a new guy at Wolfie's. Wow! For the first time in my life I understood what it meant to be "popular."

As the weeks went by the novelty of dressing up and going out every night began to wear thin. I found myself growing bored and somewhat restless. I looked forward to none of it nearly as much as I looked forward to the mail delivery bringing a letter from Karl. Before leaving Chicago I had attempted to cajole him into taking a long weekend jaunt to Florida so that we might pick up the relationship that had barely begun. I had underestimated his fear of flying. True, he had to fly while in the army but now his determination to stay on solid ground trumped his desire to see me. His letters began to take on a romantic tone. He would take his finals soon, get his medical diploma, and depart for his internship in Brooklyn. He made it clear that he did not wish to go alone. What had I done by leaving? I recalled missing my chances with Jay by running off to New York to act in stock one fateful summer.

Rather than wait for me he had hastily eloped with a hairdresser. Was history about to repeat itself?

I remained in Doris's good graces by keeping out of Thalia and Phil's way. Their romance was heating up, as was Karl's ardor. I began to feel the pressure of an ultimatum. "How long are you staying down there? I thought is was to be just a short visit." And now there was a further complication. My parents were taking a two-week vacation in Miami Beach where they would share my little apartment with me. Much as I dreaded it, I felt their arrival had an up side. I had sensed their concern in Chicago, where I had precious few dates. Now, for the first time, Mom and Daddy would see that I had boy friends and that possibly I wouldn't end up an "old maid" after all.

They arrived on a Saturday and I immediately took off on a chaste movie date with Arnie. On Sunday I left them to fend for themselves, figuring they'd be happy that I had already made a life for myself. As usual, I figured wrong. That night I came home about eleven p.m. to discover my parents were already in bed. As I tiptoed around, I heard my mother whispering in her usual *sotto* voice (which came through loud and clear), *She's just no good, Dave. She's been rotten all her life and she's not getting any better. She's a little tramp. I don't know what we're going to do with her. I should have died the day she was born.*

I froze. At the open door to the refrigerator I was about to pour a glass of milk. My knees turned to jelly. I had been the object of my mother's vitriol before, but nothing like this. I could move my arm just slightly and reach into the drawer to the right and take out the large butcher knife. Then I could grant my mother her wish. I'd sink it into her through her pink flannel nightgown before turning it on myself. Without taking a breath, I collapsed onto my sofa bed waiting to hear some defense from my father. Because of his well-modulated voice I had no way of knowing if he concurred or contradicted. I thought I heard sobs coming from his throat but I was too busy chocking down my own to be certain. What right had that woman to cause my poor Daddy such pain?

This night will mark the end of my trying to please my mother. *Here I am doing a remarkable job of teaching little Jewish children and going out on innocent dates with respectable Jewish men. What more can she ask?* I was finished.

I counted the hours until I knew Karl was awake on Pacific Standard Time before stealing down to the drug store to place the call. "I'm quitting my job. I'm coming back. Can you meet me at Union Station?"

A farewell note taped to a bathroom mirror, just like the one I had left when I ran off alone to New York City. One more nail in the parental coffin.

As the train chugged to a stop, there was Karl, a warm, welcoming smile on his face. He planted a kiss on my lips as he lifted down my luggage. True it was Chicago, but for the first time I felt as though I was home.

THE PROPOSAL

We kissed. We hugged. "Where to?" Karl asked, as he stuffed my bag into the trunk of the little Willys. Anxious to get the soot of a coach train trip off of my skin, I opted for a long soak in a tub rather than the quick shower in the jerry-rigged monstrosity in Karl's kitchen. My parents would be safely stowed in Miami Beach for nearly two more weeks, so there seemed no reason not to take advantage of their large apartment. Still somewhat cautious after running away from Florida with only a note to my father and a quick call to Thalia, I invited Karl in. Careful to tread lightly, so that our neighbors below remain oblivious, I led him to the rear of the apartment. Before I could turn the tap to fill the tub, we had fallen into the bed in my brother's old room. And there we remained for two whole days. He had no classes over the weekend; I had no desire to be anyplace but in the crook of his arm.

By the time he was ready to leave for school on Monday morning, provisions in my mother's cupboard had dwindled to the point where we braved a breakfast at the diner near my father's store on 71st. Street. During our time together I had vented my anger towards my mother. To share such an unsavory family history was a great relief. I began to feel closer to this man than to anyone I had ever known. My lack of direction, the emptiness of my life, became evident as we talked. Our lovemaking was the glue that might hold us together, but once again, my fear of losing him when he left for his internship made me unable to relax and savor the moment.

The bright chrome and red diner was all too familiar. Not only did it hold high-school memories, it was dangerously close to my father's store. Acquaintances and fellow shopkeepers often appeared on the round stools at the counter. I pulled Karl into the safety of a secluded booth at the rear. Almost at once a brassy redhead in a white uniform appeared with two cups of coffee. The large pink carnation at her lapel made a striking contrast to the hair piled high on top of her head. "What can I get you two lovebirds?" Was it that obvious?

Kellogg's corn flakes for me, eggs over easy with rye toast for him. Our order arrived in record time with a cheery, "Here you go. My name's Maggie. Let me know if you need anything else." Everything always seemed to go right with Karl, even the service in a diner.

He began talking at once with more animation than usual. As I dawdled over my corn flakes, I must have let my mind drift for I lost track of what he was saying. What was that? He was anxious about flying to the east coast, preferring, he said, to just see if the Willys would make it all the way to New York. And then I could have sworn that he used the pronoun, *we* as in "we could drive all the way and turn it into our Honeymoon."

"Honeymoon." Did that mean what I thought it meant? Was this a proposal? Was he asking me to marry him? No, no, of course not. Couldn't be a proposal.

Something didn't feel right. Wasn't I supposed to be "asked?" Wasn't I supposed to have the opportunity to say *yay* or *nay*? Careful now. Don't ask him what he means, just go along with the game.

"Everything all right here?"

"Yes, yes, Maggie. Just fine."

Karl was finishing his second cup of coffee when he casually added, "Well, if we're gonna get married, we'd better do it right away before graduation so I'll have a little free time away from the books. So how about the end of April?"

There could be no doubt. He had just used the "M" word. Careful not to move a muscle, not to break out in a grin. Careful not to hop across the table, kiss him on the mouth, ruffle his hair. Don't say a word. Stay perfectly still, or this might go away. He might break out in a laugh, assuring me that he was only teasing—that it was a colossal joke and didn't I get it? I held my breath and nodded.

"More coffee?" Maggie again.

"No thanks." It wasn't Karl's softest tone of voice. I hoped he'd never use it on me.

Where were we? "The end of April?" Casual now. Matter of fact. "Sure. That sounds good. I think I can do a wedding by the end of April."

Tossing down a bill, Karl dashed out to catch the I.C. train. Still keeping our cover, he left without so much as a peck on my cheek. Maggie took the pencil from behind her ear and scribbled the check, as she picked up the bill that Karl had left. She noticed the stunned expression on my face and saw that I had barely moved since Karl left.

A sympathetic nod, as Maggie violated the unwritten rules of waitressing by sliding into the booth next to me. She slipped an arm around me while comforting me, "It's O.K. Honey. There are plenty more fish in the sea."

Finally, I could free up the smile I had been stifling. I looked up at this big- hearted sister suddenly aware of the well-worn ring on her third finger, left hand.

"No, everything's fine, Maggie. I just got engaged … I think."

THE RING

It's Official

My parents return from Miami. I am ensconced in my old bedroom.
An uneasy, truce seems to have been declared. Not a word is mentioned
about my hasty retreat from Miami Beach. Supposedly I am job hunting
although interviews are few and far between. Every night around 6 p.m.
I take off for a date with Karl. We seem to be headed towards a wedding,
although everything remains vague. One evening he tells me that he has
just received his whopping severance pay from the army.

"I've got a check for $550.00. How would you feel about using it for
an engagement ring?"

Oh boy, oh boy, a real engagement ring at last! Memories of Jay in
Cunningham Walsh's antique jewelry store in St Louis come flooding
back. I was only eighteen, but Jay had insisted I pick out an antique ring
to signify that we would someday tie the knot. The ring I had set my heart
on was a beautiful opal. When the dowager shopkeeper had refused to sell
it to us because opals were "bad luck" Jay had lost interest. The subject
was closed, never to be re-opened. I often wondered how much more bad
luck the ring could have brought me had it gotten as far as my third finger.

"Sure, Honey, I'd love a ring. But I you know I only like antique jewelry.
I'd never wear one of those big platinum diamond monstrosities."

"Anything you want. That is, if it doesn't cost more than my army check.
An antique ring sounds great. I love all that old gold antique jewelry
you wear."

Settled! We make a date for the following afternoon to go shopping in the antique store neighborhood on Wabash Avenue. I am literally on cloud nine, but still afraid to show it around my parents. Somehow it doesn't yet feel official, it's just too good to be true.

I dress with unusual care. High heels of brown suede compliment a beige knit dress and a brown leather purse. My hair is just the right length. Looking great. I can hardly keep the smile off my face.

Unfortunately my mother hasn't yet left for her afternoon meeting. She stops me at the front door. "Where are you going all dressed up like that young lady? Are you going to see that Karl again?"

"Yeah, Mom. I'm meeting him downtown for lunch."

"Why are you wasting your time with that man? He'll never marry you, you know. And you shouldn't even want that. He's not right for you. He's already been married once and he's way too old. He'll be forty when you'll still be in your 'twenties. And when you turn forty he'll be an old man in his 'fifties!"

Shaking now. My voice unsteady. Is this the right time to break the news? I might come home with a ring on my third finger. Shouldn't wait much longer. Before she starts hollering, I open the front door and take one step out into the hallway. I turn back to face her. In case she should try to slam the door on me, I hold it in place by putting one foot inside.

"As a matter of fact, Mom. That's why I'm going downtown. I'm meeting him and we're going to look at engagement rings together. We're going to get married as soon as he finishes medical school."

A long beat as she looks at me. The furrowed brow softens. Her whole face relaxes. She suddenly loses five years. "Are you sure?"

"Absolutely. We're going to have to start planning a wedding."

"A wedding?" I can't remember hearing such excitement in her voice, ever.

She sprints to the telephone in the back of the flat, a movement somewhere between joy and panic. "I've got to call your father!"

The Lunch

Karl was to meet me at my favorite restaurant—Riccardos. If only I could have been able to have my own apartment on the Near North Side and become a regular at Riccardos I would have been content to remain in Chicago forever. I had been introduced to this Bohemian hangout, a favorite of actors and newsmen, during the days I had spent with the likes of Studs Terkel and Wyn Stracke rehearsing at *Stage for Action*. Located just under the bridge on top of which sits The Chicago Tribune and the Wrigley Buildings, the atmosphere here was a 360 degree turnaround from the eateries on 71st street in South Shore. Whenever I could, I wended my way to this restaurant, which boasted walls of brightly colored murals painted by gifted local artists. Not only did Ric Riccardo serve the best pasta in town, he had introduced me to my favorite drink. With time to spare before a radio voice-over audition one afternoon, I had stopped at the bar, hoping to calm my nerves. Ric was on duty when I expressed my desire for a dry martini, and my fear that it might make me too woozy. "Dottie," he explained, "if you want a martini, you don't have to have it with gin, you can have it with vodka. And if you don't want it with vermouth, try some of this instead. At that he brought out a bottle of a lovely deep red liquid. It was marked *Dubonnet*. I had never heard of it. Ric mixed equal parts of vodka with the red stuff, added a twist of lemon and plenty of rocks and passed it across the oak bar. One sip of this delicious concoction was enough to establish it as my drink of choice for life,

As I hurried through the door on Rush St. I had a moment of dread lest Karl had been unable to find the place or worse still, that it would not be to his liking. Wrong on both counts. Had I underestimated him? He was on a stool near the front, looking out for me while sipping a gin and tonic. He leaned over and planted a *slurpy* kiss on my cheek.

"I got here early. Guess I must be a little nervous."

"Me too. But I'm also starving. Let's eat."

Over spaghetti carbonara and a glass of wine I relayed my conversation with my mom.

"So I guess you're stuck with me now. Let's hurry. I have a list of the best jewelers on Antique Row."

The Search

We began at the north end of a block of promising looking antique shops. It wasn't St. Louis' Olive Street, but the closest thing Chicago had to offer. As we entered the first musty store, we were greeted warily by a youngish man who seemed disinterested in our mission. "I don't have anything here that would satisfy this lady for her engagement. But look around if you want to." He left us to gaze into a case of dreary rings and bracelets. Rather than evoking happy times, they all looked tired and depressing. The atmosphere was enough to deflate the bubble that had surfaced during our lunch.

"Let's get out of here!" I nudged Karl towards the door.

Three stores later I began to wonder if this idea wasn't a mistake. Each of the rings that held even the slightest appeal had a major fault: much too tight or too humungous or the stones threatening to come loose from their prongs or, indeed, already missing. Finally I tried one that was a perfect fit—a ring with a circle of five pretty blue stones across its center. I wasn't thrilled, but the need for an immediate commitment *avec* ring overpowered my better judgment. In my zeal for the deal to be finalized, perhaps I should be willing to "settle." After all, compromise was nothing new to me. Wouldn't Dr. Greene insist that I was being too picky? I held up my left hand for Karl's approval. After just a second, he responded with an unmistakable, shake of his head.

"No, no. You said you never wear blue. All wrong"

A narrow escape. Relieved, I returned the mediocre sapphires to their slot.

The shop next door held greater promise with its sign promoting "Estate Jewelry." A welcome-sounding bell tinkled as we entered and a kindly looking older man approached. "Well, I imagine you would want something with a diamond." And he brought out a black velvet tray holding an array of rings all of which boasted those sparkling clear stones. I shook my head. "It doesn't have to be a diamond. That's so corny. Let's look at those over there with red stones. My birthstone is a garnet. I've always loved them." But the garnets were chipped and dirty, most of them already coming loose.

Sensing defeat, the owner's voice took on a lively tone. "How about a ruby?" I have something that would make a beautiful engagement ring."

He disappeared into the back of the shop for a moment, returning with a lovely yellow-gold band. In its center were prongs raised high in perfect old-fashioned Tiffany style. Securely fastened was mounted a clear round sparkling stone—exactly the color of Dubonnet. As he handed it to me I took time to read the inscription inside: *Paul to Mary, Forever.* I extended my left hand and held the ring out to Karl for him to slip on my finger. It slid over my knuckles, coming to rest on my third finger as though it had always lived there.

"Do you like it?" I asked Karl, who assured me he loved it. It would appear the matter was settled. He turned to the shopkeeper and asked the price. I held my breath.

"That ring is $3,000.00, but I'm sure we could come down a little for you." We both tried to hide our shock.

"I'm afraid that's a little out of my price range" muttered poor Karl, before being treated to a lesson in precious gems.

"A perfect ruby is one of the rarest and most precious of stones. This one is unusual in its size and clarity and its color. I suppose I could let it go for $2,500.00, and you'd be getting a real bargain."

Our $550.00 check shrunk like a cheap suit. We were drained, the fun and excitement of the search suddenly over.

"Let's call it a day."

The Pre-Nup Dinner

The atmosphere in our apartment on Clyde Avenue had never been so charged. When Daddy returned from work that evening, in a rare outburst of physical affection, he actually kissed me. It was always hard for my father to express his sentiments, but when I saw that his eyes were moist, I realized the extent of his emotions.

"Are you happy, Do?" he wanted to know. "How well do you know Karl? When do we get to meet him?"

My mother had beaten him to the punch: "He's coming to dinner tomorrow night. Tell me what he eats. Dorothy, do you think he'd like my brisket?"

Oh, no, not that overcooked piece of dry beef that my mother thought of as one of her specialties. Not wishing to throw a damper on the important dinner, I assured her it was one of his favorites. "Be forewarned," I cautioned Karl. "My whole family tells her they love it. Even my Aunt Flo, her own sister, doesn't have the heart to tell her how long she overcooks it."

"Relax, Honey. I can't wait to meet them. We'll get through it and I promise to behave."

He promises to behave? I don't dare let him know that compared with the one disastrous meal at which I shared a serious boyfriend with my parents, he could not help but pass with flying colors. Jay had appeared at his inspection evening in an outfit years ahead of its time, a cross somewhere between the John Lennon and Mr. Rogers. The bizarre get-up coupled with unwanted revelations about his occupation ("I make crystal chandeliers and I publish an *avant-garde* magazine") had completely flummoxed my poor father—the Beau Brummell of South Shore.

Flo tried to horn in. She felt she really should be present to inspect the new merchandise. Her sister Lily, however, had different ideas. For once she would be the star of the show.

Twenty minutes before he was scheduled to arrive, the telephone rang. "Sorry, Honey. The surgery rounds lasted way late. I'm on my way, but I didn't have time to change."

"Doesn't matter, Karl. Just get here!"

When our front doorbell rang, I opened it to see my handsome prince standing there in rumpled white jacket and pants. A stethoscope peeked out of his right pocket. As icing on the cake, there was even a drop of blood splattered on his lapel as if "straight from wardrobe." If my mother knew how to swoon, she would have done so on the spot. For here, in our dining room, flashing a warm smile, stood "my son-in-law the doctor!" He graciously poured the wine he had remembered to bring, raised his glass in a toast to his new family, then polished off a plate of brisket, mashed potatoes with gravy, and peas. My nerves began to settle. As my mother and I were clearing plates, I heard my father grilling Karl about his background. His father, who had recently died, had been a well-known doctor in Rock Island, Illinois. His sister and her husband were believed to own half of that town. I wasn't worried.

Over the canned peaches and raspberry *rugalla*, Daddy got down to business: "So, Lil tells me you are looking at engagement rings. Where did you shop?"

We launched into the saga of our search on Wabash Avenue, forced to admit we had not yet succeeded.

"Listen, kids. I hesitate to interfere, but you shouldn't waste Karl's army pay on some old piece of junk. Nate Roth's son-in-law has a fine wholesale jewelry business in the 29 East Madison building. Make an appointment, go see him, he'll make anything you want for you, and he'll give you a good deal. He's honest and you'll be getting something new and shiny that will last you forever." To my father, *new and shiny* was the future. *Old* was the past. *Old* meant Eastern Europe and pogroms. *New* was his family and his successful haberdashery business.

My fiancé (for it was now official) looked at me and nodded, "Sounds like a good idea. Let's go Wednesday on my day off."

His enthusiasm made it clear. He really didn't want me wearing somebody else's old ring. *Old* was his first marriage gone bad. It was Pearl Harbor and Okinawa, not an imagined charming legacy handed down to the grandchildren of *Paul and Mary*. He had just gone along with the idea to please me. Karl was not Jay and it was time I realized it, accepted it.

So that was how we came to "Harold Berland, Wholesale Jewelers" in the East Madison Building, and to a four-fifths of a carat diamond.

Four-Fifths of a Carat

The following Wednesday we dispensed with the preliminaries, skipping lunch and getting right down to business. 29 East Madison was in Chicago's financial district, an imposing skyscraper in stark contrast to the musty antique shops that held such an air of mystery and excitement for me. As we waited for the elevator in the marble lobby, I had a nagging feeling that I was "selling out." I looked up at the tall, handsome almost-doctor beside me and took his hand in mine, giving it a loving squeeze. In return I was rewarded with a second or two of light pressure. Compromise, according to Dr. Greene, was the name of the game, and I would begin by giving this man whatever he wanted as long as he didn't renege on his promise to make an "honest woman" of me.

I had met Harold Berland once or twice following his marriage to the daughter of my father's best friend. Now he greeted me in his pristine little jewelry shop with a warm hug, a handshake to Karl, and a hearty *Mazel-tov.*

We told Harold the amount of Karl's check, half expecting him to scoff. On the contrary, he was certain he could make us an engagement ring we will love. The glittering platinum and jeweled pieces on display made me cringe. I was not quite ready to relinquish all of my power just yet.

"Harold, I have to warn you—I only like antique jewelry. These are very pretty, but I can't imagine wearing any of the rings I see here in this case."

"I understand. No problem. If you like antique, you probably just want a simple gold band with a single diamond set in a traditional Tiffany setting. Something like this."

He brought out exactly the gold ring I had in mind. The difference was, this one was shiny and smooth, its high raised prongs ready to embrace a precious stone.

"How did you know? That's *exactly* what I want. Perfect!"

That being settled, he turned to the would-be groom. Karl assured him that really wanted me to have a diamond and hoped that could be achieved with his $550.00 army check. Harold disappeared into his vault and returned with little bags of what seemed like chips of glass. Spreading them on a throw of black velvet, he separated five or six from the rest of the pile. Then he took out one of those little circular glass magnifying glasses and inserted it into his eye.

"Here are two that fit your pocketbook and they are both lovely stones. Would you like to see how they really look inside?"

I bent my head, squinted one eye, and looked through the little magnifying glass just like an expert. Almost at once I was rewarded with dancing lights and colors that I had never dreamed could exist in a diamond. Karl and I took turns with the glass, having the fun we had missed on Wabash Avenue. Finally the choice narrowed down to two.

"This one's a little bigger," Harold explained. "It's a perfect diamond although its color is a bit on the yellow side. Now this one is a fraction smaller, just about 4/5 of a carat, but it is what is known as a blue diamond. Many experts feel that is the most coveted. Very clear, nearly blue when you look closely."

Karl and I looked at one another. "Let's take it," our eyes said. Then Harold interrupted, "I must tell you, though, this lovely diamond has a flaw. If you look very closely you'll see a slight crack running down its center."

Squinting into the magnifying glass, I caught sight of what he meant. An almost imperceptible thread ran through my otherwise perfect diamond.

"Will this hurt anything? Will it ever crack in two?"

"I assure you, nothing will ever happen to it and no one will ever know it's there. Most jewelers wouldn't have even told you. So what do you think? You and Karl take your time. Choose the one you want. You can't go wrong with either one. I can have your ring made up for you by the beginning of the week."

He left us alone to ponder our first major mutual decision. The little blue diamond really spoke to me, but would it be bad luck to begin my marriage with a crack? Nothing is ever perfect for me. I decided to place the final decision in the hands of my future husband.

Karl opted for the blue diamond, flaw and all. We had just enough money left to have Harold make up two heavy, plain gold wedding bands, perfect imitations of those worn for generations before, but new and shiny, just like our future.

WEDDING PLANS

World War II had broken out, as I was about to graduate high school. For the next few years, most of the eligible young men would be drafted, many would serve overseas. Suddenly my peers were getting married and more alarming still, they were becoming mothers while still in their 'teens. My parents had spent years brainwashing me against this scenario. *Don't marry young, get an education first* was the mantra drilled into me over and over. Like a dutiful daughter I went to university and got my degree. I steered clear of soldiers and sailors, making sure all my boyfriends were medically excused from combat by what was known as *4-F.* I held nothing but contempt for those who had dropped out of school to wash diapers. I had sweated out four years of term papers and exams only to emerge with a piece of parchment, but where was the wedding ring that was supposed to be waiting as I threw my cap in the air?

The four years since my graduation had presented my parents with nothing but grief. Over and over they were besieged with the same question: "So, what's new with Dorothy? So, has she met anyone yet?" A knife cutting into my poor mama's heart. Now's her chance to get even.

"At last," she told me, "it's my turn. Finally all the wedding gifts I have given all these years will be repaid. Finally I can wear a *mother of the bride* dress."

"No, no, I'm not going to walk down an aisle and give all those people the chance to gloat over the fact that your daughter has finally made a catch. No, I'll have a little wedding, but it will just be for our close family. We cut off the list at first cousins. No friends. No friends allowed."

In one fell swoop my edict eliminated all the Sadies and Ethels and Esthers and their families. However I was true to my word. What's good for one is good for all. So that meant no Cynthia, no Paula, no Thalia, no Bunny. The list was written in stone. No children, no friends, and (although I failed to realize it) no fun.

We were pressed for time. Karl's internship in Brooklyn would begin in a few short weeks. Israel was just becoming a state and all Jewish weddings were banned during the exact dates that would have worked. Since my needs were simple, we were able to secure the venue (The Windermere East Hotel) and a caterer on short notice. I agreed that our elderly Rabbi Teller should officiate. Next on the agenda was the question of what to wear.

"We'll go to the bridal shop next to Daddy's store. They've already picked out a few in your size."

"Absolutely not! No white! No bridal gown! I won't have people snickering!"

So, no white. No train. No veil. No pretty.

THE BRIDAL DRESS

My Aunt Flo's husband Eddie had an aunt and uncle who owned a large dress shop on the west side of Chicago. It would be worth the trip, for not only was Sacks Fashion Shop known for its stylish clothes, but of course, we would get everything "strictly wholesale."

Eddie's unmarried sister, fashionable redheaded Aunt Miriam, greeted us.

"So, Do, you're beating me to the *chupah*. If you're really set against a bridal gown, you should try these dresses that we just got in. They're made of a new material called *polyester*. It won't wrinkle, and it is even washable." Miriam brought out a few dresses made of a sheer fabric comprised of puffy little squares. This new lightweight material had a certain appeal. On my way to one of Sack's luxurious dressing rooms, I am accosted by the owner herself, the buxom, thickly accented Manya Sacks. *Mazel tov* to my mother. Then she turns to me. "So who are you marrying?"

What a busybody! As if she'd know my finance, the son of a prestigious doctor from The Tri-Cities of Iowa and Illinois.

"You don't know him."

"Try me. Who is he?"

"You couldn't know him."

"Try me."

"His name is Karl Friedman and he goes to the University of Illinois Medical School and he's from Rock Island."

Manya shot back. "Karl Friedman? From Rock Island? No, no, I don't know him. Not much I don't know him. He was born on the Northwest side, no?"

"I think so."

"No, no, I don't know him. Only since he was one day old. I only took his mother, Mary, on the streetcar to the hospital the night he was born. But no, I don't know him."

Mary? She must be remembering correctly. The story came back to me—how his own father had a delivery that night so a neighbor had taken his mother, to the hospital where she promptly gave birth to her youngest child, a boy.

So much for my longed-for anonymity. My mother's face lit up like the Wrigley Building at night.

"You know his family?"

As Manya related more details of the clan I was about to join, Mom breathed an audible sigh of relief. All the credentials in the world had not assured her of my intended's pedigree until now. Manya Sacks had succeeded in legitimizing the Herman Friedmans of Rock Island.

"Wait until I tell Dave and Florence. Wait until the girls hear this at mahjong. Miriam, make sure Dorothy gets something pretty. It's all right if it's expensive."

Too late. I was already fixated on a light blue puffy polyester that ended just below my knees. Little black velvet buttons ran down its front, a black velvet belt circled my non-too-tiny waist. I knew that black was considered *verboten* for a bride. Miriam suggested replacing the belt and buttons, but by wearing the black, I was flaunting my rebellion against those middle class values I had fought hard to escape. I was also opting for my least flattering color. So, no white, no long, no veil, no pretty. The perfect compromise.

THE WEDDING

May 6, 1950, five o'clock p.m. The small ballroom in the Windermere East Hotel is set with round tables, each seating eight members of assorted Friedmans and Sapers. The "no children" rule has been eased to include Aunt Flo's kids, Gene and Janet, who are now fourteen and ten as well as five year-old Arthur, Karl's adorable nephew, who will act as ring-bearer. Sure, including this little kid is a concession but I tell myself that is a good political move that will endear me to the groom's family. The room adjoining the ballroom will host the ceremony itself.

Daddy pulls his Buick around the circular driveway and lets me out before depositing it with the doorman. As usual, there is a gusty wind blowing off of nearby Lake Michigan. It plays havoc with my hair (one more reason to leave Chicago without regret). I hang on tightly to the little "Juliet Cap" with its short veil that I have had made to match my pastel polyester dress. The high heels that have been tinted the exact shade of blue are already beginning to hurt.

My Mother helps me through the heavy swinging glass doors into the lobby. Because it is located south of the Loop, in Hyde Park, the Windermere is the poor man's version of the snazzy Drake Hotel on North Michigan Blvd. My teeth are chattering. On this blustery spring evening, why is the air conditioning turned up full blast? Can't Chicago get anything right? I look around for Karl but there is no sign of him nor anyone else from his family. I begin to shiver. Could my worst fantasy be coming true? Has he had second thoughts? It's been nearly 24 hours since we last spoke. Enough time for him to have decided not to go through with it. Tales of brides left waiting at the alter run through my head. This could turn into the very worst thing that has ever happened to me. I knew it was too good to be true, but what have I done to deserve this? How could anyone have been so cruel? Perhaps this was why Bernice was trying to warn me that Karl was not good marriage material. I will not even try putting on a good face for my guests, who might be parking their cars at this very moment. If the wedding is off, I will do an about-face, push the swinging doors against the wind and fight my way into one of the waiting taxis in front of the hotel. I will have the driver take me straight to the Greyhound terminal where I will board a bus for St. Louis. It doesn't matter that Jay has married someone else, it will be enough just to be near him. Never, never will I set foot in Chicago, Illinois again!wind - fight

The official bridal planner from the hotel bursts forth, a look of relief crossing her face. "Hurry, we're waiting for you! We expected you a half-hour ago!" On this, the most important day of my life, I have managed to be late. Can't even blame my mother. My fault for fussing too long with my hair. Miss Wedding Planner ushers me into a small anteroom where good old Rabbi Teller is seated at a carved desk. Atop his head is perched a high square black *yarmulke* just like the one he wore long ago at Flo and Eddie's wedding. It looks a little worn. Could it be the same one? Has he been too broke or too lazy or too superstitious to replace it after all these years? To his left stands the man who will soon become my husband. Carl Martin Friedman. Before the day is over I will be Mrs. Carl M. Friedman! He is wearing an unfamiliar white satin skullcap that is listing slightly to the left. He is smiling. He looks up. He sees me. The smile turns broader. Could he, too, be relieved when I showed up? I raise my head for a peck on my cheek. Instead he surprises me with a kiss on my lips. My father takes this in. He beams. His little girl is going to be all right. He has deposited the car and made his way in for the signing of the *katuba* (the marriage contract). I seem to recall that parents are not supposed to be permitted at this ceremony, but I don't care. What is a broken rule compared with the overdue happiness of my Daddy? My face feels flushed. The crisis has passed. My feet no longer hurt. I am living proof of the phrase, *trembling with joy.*

I realize a pre-ceremony sighting of the bride is against custom, but since there is nothing customary about this wedding, I decide to circulate among the guests as they nibble hors d'oeuvres. I assume the role of gracious hostess rather than nervous bride. I am particularly ingratiating to everyone on the groom's side, whom I consider more sophisticated, intelligent, affluent, artistic, and politically aware than mine. I attempt to charm the dowager of the family, maiden Aunt Millie, who has traveled alone all the way from Los Angeles for the occasion. At the advanced age of sixty-five this is considered quite a feat. She takes my hand for a moment, but the frozen smile and the modulated tone of voice assure me that I have a long way to go before earning her total approval. When I turn my attention to the relatives on Daddy's side, my cousin Frankie rushes over to pump my hand and grin at me as he pecks my cheek, mouthing some unintelligible words. I am not certain how to respond. Frank was born deaf and has never been able to speak clearly enough for me to understand. His two sisters and his father, my Uncle Itzak, have all mastered sign language allowing them full access to Frankie's thoughts. Even though he is not a blood relative to her, Aunt Flo, whose high school chum was deaf, is able to communicate by signing, but I have been too lazy or too thoughtless to even know the most rudimentary phrases. I can do little more than return a stupid grin and handshake. I glance surreptitiously to the Friedman side of the room, curious about their reaction. Could they possibly imagine that Karl's bride carries a genetic weakness? Why do I continue to regard Frank as an outcast when I myself have often felt that way around my family? I feel a tap on my shoulder from my cousin Bea from Joliet who, though exactly my age, has already been married forever. She and her husband, her high school sweetheart, are wearing their usual bland expressions, but even Bea starts to chat in sign language with our mutual cousin Frank.

Relief comes in the person of Karl's beautiful younger sister, Mindelle, who sidles up to embrace me. Her natural blonde hair is pulled back into a stylish chignon, her black and white dress flatters her svelte figure which is kept intact by the many hours she spends on a North Shore golf course. Now Mindelle is introducing me to the third sister, Belle, who has long ago been diagnosed with some sort of mental illness. Belle seems just a bit off center, as she plants a kiss on my cheek. Her speech is barely audible and pitched at least an octave above the norm. No one gathers around Belle and I realize that here too is an outcast in what I want to believe is my picture-perfect new family.

Time to begin. The room actually looks pretty—as though a wedding is about to take place. White carnations are scattered about. A shimmering white runner in the center divides the space. Like the Montagues and Capulets, our two clans have seated themselves on opposite sides. The simple *chupa* is being held by my mother's younger brother and Karl's handsome brothers-in-law. Why hadn't I had the foresight and decency to honor and include Cousin Frankie by inviting him to hold one corner?

At the rear of the room I take my father's arm while I wait for the musical signal to begin. There is to be no wedding march, of course, but I have agreed that Karl's nephew Alan, a remarkable pianist, should play some Schubert. I wonder if my culture-deprived family recognizes his talent. Do they understand that I would not permit just *anybody* to play for this momentous occasion? My father is about to walk me down the aisle. My mother and brother are already standing under the *chupa* together with Eva, the elder sister who raised Karl, and her husband Izzie. Alan's baby brother, little Arthur, follows. He makes a splendid ring-bearer, careful to hold our ersatz antiques in place on top of a satin pillow. In his little plaid jacket and bow tie and short pants he comes dangerously close to stealing the show.

Alan plays beautifully and just as the music ends Eva raises a delicate lace hanky to wipe her watery eyes and turns to her husband. "It's so wonderful. I can't believe this is really happening!" Eva obviously belongs to my mother's school of the *sotto-voce*. Her relief that her youngest brother is not marrying another *shiksa* is heard by one and all. As Karl places the plain gold wedding band on my finger I have an epiphany—he has been as much of a worry to his family as I to mine. He's relieved that this will soon be over. As a matter of fact, relief is palpable on both sides of the aisle.

Now Karl stamps on the wine glass, and as it breaks, little Arthur pipes up in a voice obviously not intended to be *sotto-voce* at all, "I now pronounce you meat balls and spaghetti!" Even I am delighted at the laughter that follows. The broad smile I wear as I march up the white satin runner with my arm linked through that of my new husband is genuine. Maybe this wedding is going to be fun after all.

HONEYMOON ROAD TRIP

To nobody's surprise Karl passes his finals and can now truthfully be termed a "real doctor." Since the wedding announcements have gone to press before his official graduation, it would be dishonest, he insists, to permit my mother the joy of adding the coveted *M.D.* after his name. She must make do with the usual *Mr.* thereby failing to elevate her status above that of her assorted lady friends. Truthfully I am the tiniest bit disappointed, yet I applaud his decision. *What a wonderful, pure, ethical man I am marrying. It must be a result of his Marxist background.*

In the opinions of various automobile mechanics, it would be foolhardy to challenge the vintage Willys to make it to Brooklyn. Daddy also puts his foot down, and then surprises us with a wedding gift of a shiny new blue two-door Chevrolet sedan, the first off the assembly line since WW II. Thanks to his long-standing relationship with a customer who owned the Drexel Chevrolet Company in Hyde Park, my father had been bumped to the head of the long wait list. In keeping with his custom of buying only for cash, he writes a check in his beautiful Eastern Europe script to for the exact sum of $1,769.78. This includes the addition of $175.00 to the original purchase price for a radio, a heater, and seat covers. The automobile is one more way to secure his daughter's future happiness. As for the Willys, Karl's Rock Island boyhood chum Arty has always coveted it. For the sum of $50.00, the pink slip is now his.

Never were two people happier to cross the Illinois border and leave Chicago behind. On the outskirts of Indiana we stop at the first motel flashing a VACANCY sign. No need to slink down low and wait in the car as I have done many times before. I'm a married woman! When Karl marches into the office and registers us as "Dr. and Mrs." I stand by his side, brazenly flashing my diamond ring. Attempting to stifle a yawn, the clerk barely looks up.

We had decided on a route that would take us through Cleveland, Ohio, so that Karl could have a reunion with Jack Chernin, his old army buddy, who was just beginning private practice as a podiatrist. In a comfortable little house in an area known as "Cleveland Heights" we drank coffee and ate pie, soaking up the atmosphere of suburbia. The Chernins displaced their baby girl to give us her bedroom for the night. Too inhibited to make love in such small quarters, I couldn't wait to push on to our own nest. On our way out of town early the following morning we tacitly agreed that there was no need to ever visit Ohio again. Smugly, we congratulated ourselves on being able to start our new lives close to the bustle of New York City. As the miles flew by I made the mistake of musing aloud on an acting career. "Maybe if I don't get a full time job right away, I could take the subway into Manhattan and do some rounds one or two days a week." The decelerating power of the new Chevy was put to the test. Karl slammed on the brakes, turning to me in the parking lot of a Dairy Queen. "I thought you had gotten that out of your system. You told me you were finished with all that. I thought you agreed that we should start a family right away. You meant that, didn't you? You are through with all that, aren't you?"

His voice took on a vaguely familiar tone that I couldn't quite place though I was certain I had heard it before. Then it hit me. Of course! It was the tone Karl had used on the waitress who had annoyed him in the 71st Street diner. For a second I thought he might be kidding, but the steely expression on his face assured me this was no laughing matter. "Tell me now," the look threatened, "before we go any further."

I was on thin ice. I had survived the proposal, the wedding, and one half of a honeymoon. I had believed I was more than ready to trade in uncertainties of my old life for a secure place beside a good man. Now the ice threatened to shatter beneath me, plunging me into a cold abyss from which there might be no escape. This was the point of no return. I suddenly had the horrific feeling that I had forgotten my lines. I was buying time. This pause was too long. Then the words of my script clearly appeared before me. I found my voice, its tone reeking of a conviction that surprised me. I took Karl's hand as I assured him, "I *did* mean what I told you. I *am* through with 'all that.' Of course I've left all that behind. Now come on. Let's go in so that I can taste my first Dairy Queen!"

Karl, The Perfect Match

Do plays new housewife, Chicago
Karl in front of his apartment

Graduation Day from Med School

Honeymoon Road Trip Outside the "Dairy Queen"

Dottie and Thalia, Miami Beach

PART TWO:

BROOKLYN, NY

HONEYMOON HOTEL

As the Chevy sedan crossed the Brooklyn Bridge I turned for a final look at the Manhattan skyline. I couldn't quite shake the nagging feeling that I had unfinished business around Times Square. The promise made to Karl outside of the Ohio Dairy Queen ran through my mind but I wisely kept those thoughts to myself as I focused on what lay ahead. My first-hand knowledge of Brooklyn was limited to a day three years before when my friend Geraldine had steered me though the IRT to a murky surgeon's office on Ocean Parkway, where he assured me he would "take care of everything." Now I entered that borough as a stranger about to make it her home.

The moment my place as an intern's wife was assured I had contacted Cynthia, my best friend since college. Between us there was no favor too great to ask. A sophisticated, savvy Manhattan native, Cynthia knew all there was to know about New York, all five boroughs. Or so I thought.

In the three years since I left Greenwich Village, little had changed in the housing market—apartments were still scarce and those that were available were way beyond our price range. I gazed now at the lovely tree-lined streets and the many stately old mansions of Brooklyn Heights. There was greenery all around, kids on roller skates, and diners sipping coffee on sidewalks in front of little cafes. I could be happy here. Too soon the scenery shifted. Leafy trees were replaced by vacant lots and front yards in dire need of weeding. I opened our Thomas Guide and in a few moments we pulled up in front of the ancient Kings County Hospital, a behemoth at which Karl would spend most of his time for the next twelve months. There would be no Brooklyn Heights for us. An intern's salary was a token $25.00 a month for which he would be on call 24/7. Karl and I would coast on his small inheritance from his father plus some cash wedding gifts until I was able to find a job to supplement this income. Not only had I commissioned Cynthia to find us our first apartment, but one within our price range and close to the hospital to boot. I had not the slightest doubt that she would deliver. Sure enough, following quickly on the heels of my request came her letter describing the top floor of a converted brownstone. *Converted brownstone.* Nothing in Chicago had ever been described this way. The words echoed with romance. The landlord would graciously hold the apartment for us with the proviso that he receive two month's rent plus a security deposit in advance. A check went out *poste haste*. Back came a receipt via return mail. We were all set.

Since the apartment was leased as furnished, we had only to carry enough clothes and accessories for our immediate needs, yet the trunk of the Chevy was so tightly packed we feared to open it lest another knick knack tumble out. We couldn't wait to unpack. Our instructions were to contact the landlord, Mr. deLyra, when we found ourselves about an hour away. He would meet us, give us the keys and settle us in our apartment.

After reconnoitering around the hospital, we agreed it was time to put in the call, which I placed from a pay phone in the hot sticky lobby. No answer. Several more attempts failed. Was it possible that Cynthia had given us the wrong number? We tried again at a Brooklyn Deli, which mercifully was air-conditioned. Still no answer. Two cups of coffee later we decided to navigate on our own to our new address. The sun was starting to set when we pulled up in front of an old brownstone which, to my disappointment, proved to be not brown at all but rather a depressing grey. Too much coffee had put me in dire need of a bathroom. We tried our luck from another pay phone, this time at the corner candy store where the buxom owner took pity on me, permitting me to pull back the muslin curtain that hid her living quarters and make use of her private facilities. Five rings, and Mr. deLyra answered, assuring us he would arrive within fifteen minutes. As we walked back to our new address I put on a happy face, but forty-five minutes later my high spirits had evaporated. Somehow I couldn't help but feel this was all Karl's fault, despite the fact that more than once he had referred to my *best friend* Cynthia with a biting tongue. There was little to do except to gaze in silence at the corner, as one car after another turned onto our street and whizzed by. Any more talk and our first truly big argument was certain to erupt. A large silver Cadillac pulled up just across the street at last. Our new landlord, surely! But when a couple with a little girl slammed the car door and entered a different house, I had trouble fighting back tears. I was correct not to expect any comforting words from Karl, who remained rigid and tightlipped. Fifteen excruciating minutes later a battered green pickup truck ground to a halt at the curb and our new landlord materialized. We shook hands with this olive skinned man who announced he was indeed deLyra. I fixed my eyes on his three-day-old stubble and his mane of greasy black hair, which was almost as thick as his Brooklyn accent. Not exactly the successful real estate magnet of my imagination. From a large circular ring hanging around his belt he extracted two small keys and handed them to Karl. "Follow me, and I'll show you the *apahtment*."

When he pushed open the front door, and I was immediately treated to the strong odor of boiling cabbage. Hoping it would not drift up to the second floor, I followed my new landlord up a flight of stairs carpeted in a soiled musty brown. At the top of the landing, Mr. deLyra turned sharply to the right, although no compass was needed to know that the front of the building was to our left. "The *apahtment* was *paht* of an old mansion. They divided it into two upstairs and two downstairs. Yours is in the rear, so it faces the *gahden*."

When he unlocked the door, offering me a glimpse inside, it was a struggle to hide the shock that surely must have registered on my face. Yes, the upstairs had been divided by what appeared to be a piece of heavy cardboard nailed right down the middle. A gas range and rusty sink dominated the room, which was obviously the original kitchen. A window badly in need of washing revealed the *garden*—a sad patch of dry grass surrounded by a chain link fence. I had hoped at least for a *Tree That Might Have Grown in Brooklyn*. Turning to inspect the room I beheld a small table covered in flowered oilcloth and two formica chairs. This completed the dining area. A few feet away one overstuffed easy chair sat facing, a double bed that was pushed up against the cardboard "wall." *Nice, isn't it?* queried our landlord. He had to be kidding. Trying to hide my disappointment from Karl, who seemed unperturbed, I gamely inquired about the bathroom. Perhaps all the expense and care in remodeling had been lavished there. Perhaps it would be all new shiny silver and chrome and tile. Mr. deLyra opened the door and walked back towards the staircase. "It's right down here. Only a few steps away from your *apahtment*." A bathroom out in the hall? Not since my furnished room on West 72nd St., as a newly arrived struggling New York actress had I been subjected to such an indignity. Clinging to hope for a happy ending, I wondered why the bathroom door was closed and why deLyra peered in so cautiously. "See? A nice big tub with a *showah*."

I'd make do if I really had to, but I was annoyed to notice that the room had not been thoroughly cleaned prior to our arrival, for peeking out of a plastic cup, were two toothbrushes, a yellow and a blue. "I see that the last tenants forgot to take their toothbrushes." deLyra lowered his voice: "Those belong to the people in the front *apahtment*. You'll be sharing the bathroom with them. Did Miss Cynthia forget to tell you?"

Miss Cynthia had most certainly forgotten to mention this detail. Sharing the top floor with a family separated only by a thin wall was one thing, but I was hardly prepared for the sharing of a bathroom. It was quite possible that I would never speak to Miss Cynthia again as long as I lived.

My new husband, Defender of the Masses, was willing to give the deLyra dwelling a try. "We can fix it up a little, Do. It's near the hospital and it might not be so bad once we get used to it." *Easy for you,* I thought. *You'll see precious little of the inside of the place. You'll be on call, busy day and night in your chosen profession. If I am to be denied a life in the theatre, if that is truly out of my system at least allow me decent surroundings.*

Gamely, I had spent the first month of my married life sharing the tiny apartment that had housed Karl throughout medical school. I had developed a backache from snuggling up close on his cot-sized bed, I had exchanged my leisurely bubble baths for stingy showers in the jerry-rigged overhead shower in his kitchen, I had learned to light the pilot light on his ancient gas stove without incinerating my hair, but those weeks were filled with the heady excitement of being newly married.

Those had been temporary "honeymoon" weeks that would end when my "real" life began. *Certainly*, I thought, *compared to what you are used to this place is a palace, but sharing a toilet with strangers was not what I signed on for.* Karl, on the other hand, had survived a war in the Pacific, he had organized labor unions in the coal mines of West Virginia; a shared bathroom was not about to daunt him. He tried to reason with his Princess Bride from South Shore. "Dorothy, a lot of money is tied up here. Let's just give it a try."

Financial negotiation with the apartment owner appeared highly unlikely. "Gotta go now" he told us with a grin as he bounded down the steps and into his truck. I watched as he gunned the engine and rounded the corner, disappearing in a cloud of dust, our first and last month's rent in hand. I wanted to shout, "Stop, come back, that's my future you're driving off with!" Instead I stood motionless, my mind flashing on the many disappointments I had experienced in my life. I didn't want to leave Karl and yet I could not face going back upstairs. I opened my purse and felt for a pristine twenty-dollar bill that I had tucked away inside the zippered pocket as "mad money." One night. One night only. That is my limit. Tomorrow if he insists on staying here I'll call a taxi and leave. (Calling a taxi and running away was proving to be my favorite fantasy.) The bill was my exit ticket—it could carry me back across the bridge to Cynthia's or Geraldine's or Tashka's where I was certain to be welcomed. Night settled in; street lamps were lit. There was no choice but to drag a few necessities up the two flights of stairs. Plopping down on the dingy easy chair, with a sigh of resignation I pulled some slippers from my overnight case and padded down to the communal bathroom. I turned the doorknob only to hear a booming masculine voice from inside: "Just a minute!" I raced back to the sanctuary of our converted kitchen, where it was impossible to stifle my tears. Hoping that sleep would release me from this nightmare, I slid under the strange linens, turning to the wall, my back to my bridegroom. To my surprise, he climbed onto his side of the bed and wrapped his arms around me in spoon fashion, immediately becoming aroused. Just moments before, making love would have been out of the question, but suddenly hot sex seemed like a good idea. As I turned to respond, the wall behind us (which I later learned was made of a new material called *masonite*) began a distinctive, rhythmical shake. The banging lasted only a few moments and was quickly replaced by unmistaken voices of a male and a female. Almost at once they were followed by what sounded like a hiccup or a cough, and next a loud wail. *Waa, waa, waa*!! It wasn't possible, or was it? It seemed our neighbors had come equipped with a newborn infant, one that refused to be quieted for the next two hours.

So much for sex, so much for sleep. By morning, bleary-eyed and frustrated, the doctor was ranting at his landlord, at his wife and at her "best friend" Cynthia. Everything was my fault. "Do you realize that I'll be on call at the hospital every other night? Do you realize that I've got to be able to have a good night's sleep when I get home? Do you realize that I could kill a patient if I was overtired? Do you realize that lack of sleep could flunk me right out of my internship?"

"Yes, Karl, I do. But do you realize that I won't survive if I am forced to spend my life in these surroundings?"

Oblivious to the fact that we had raised our voices to a level that could be overheard, we were stopped short by another set of "*Waa, waa, waa*s." We had succeeded in awakening the sleeping baby. No need to hassle any longer. We returned to the deli for breakfast where I was able to make out the words of the assertive Karl, he of the domineering voice, on the phone with deLyra making threatening demands that surprised even me. Neither soiled toothbrushes nor a cardboard partition had done the trick, but a crying infant proved to be my salvation.

Concealing my smug smile I opened the throwaway newspaper and began scouring the want ads listing "Apartments for Rent."

HUNTING FOR HOUSING

The search for suitable housing was on. Brooklyn Eagle in hand, we began the hunt with addresses nearest Kings County Hospital, fanning out from there. As we rejected one miserable place after another, my empathy for Cynthia grew. Although I had assigned her an impossible task she had been unwilling to admit defeat. My circle of friends from Madison had always believed that no favor was too great to ask of one another. (Such loyalty, I might add, has persisted throughout our lives) Karl's internship would begin in just two days. We were running out of time.

Now Karl had the bright idea of stopping at the hospital to look at a bulletin board where housing for staff was posted. Waving a scrap of paper, he returned to the car with a smile on his formerly glum face.

"Do, this one sounds really promising. It's not a walkup, but a walk-down. A newly converted furnished basement apartment in the home of a quiet couple and it's really close to the hospital. I just spoke to Mrs. Rubin the owner and she's expecting us. Let's get going before someone beats us to it."

A couple in their late 'seventies answers the doorbell of their red brick house the moment we ring. Their eyes light up at the sight of an appealing, possibly Jewish, young couple. Introductions are made and like my mother, Mrs. Rubin comes close to swooning at the thought of a doctor sharing her home. "You must be anxious to see the place." She points to a door just inside their front door. We can go down through this closet right here or we can walk around to the side of the house. Leo and I decided there would be more privacy if we had an outside entrance put in. You'll see. You'll have your own private entrance with your own lock and key."

Mrs. Rubin opens the door of what appears to be a guest closet and lo and behold, a staircase leading to what formerly must have been a cellar. "Why bother to walk around?" says Faye, "Here, we can just go down these steps." *Oh, so these nice people could just walk down a flight of steps to enter our apartment any time they felt like it.*

Leo remained on his sofa. In mere seconds we descended into what may well become our final honeymoon home. My future landlady proudly showed off the new shower, the new stove and refrigerator, the new mattress, the new curtains framing the high little basement windows. The place had a warm, inviting look. We discussed money. I was painfully aware that rent prices had been steadily climbing since we had moved away from DeLyra's. So anxious was Faye to have us as her first tenants that she immediately came down five dollars a month. Our enthusiasm indicated that things were nearly settled. Then she played what she thought was her trump card.

"You like soup? I cook soup twice a veek and I could make extra and bring a pot down for you. You're going to be all alone vile your husband is at vork? I'm home a lot so vee could visit together. Here, you vouldn't be lonely. You'd be like my own daughter."

Where was that outside exit? I spotted a heavy door just next to the kitchen sink and pushed Karl towards it. "Thanks, Mrs. Rubin. Sounds great. We have just one more place to look at before we decide. Karl, we'd better leave now or we'll be late." Brazenly turning the knob I nudged him out of what luckily proved to be the outside door.

As I settled into the Chevy I take a last look at Faye Rubin waving from the entrance of what I see as more a prison than a home. I hadn't married and left Chicago to become a roommate of another Manya Sacks. No way would my compromise include Grandma Faye and her chicken soup. Thankfully, Karl too, had his own fantasies of nights with his bride and they did not include worrying about the Rubins listening above. I urged Karl to drive off quickly lest Mrs. Rubin dash out with another tempting offer.

I turned to the Want Ad page where several notices were already obliterated by heavy X's. My eyes kept wandering to the large advertisement at the bottom of the page: "Brand New Modern Apartments. Unfurnished. Kings Highway. Immediate Occupancy"

"Brand new" resonated with an appealing sound. The wedding gifts in the trunk of our car were new, as was the diamond on my third finger left hand. Our blue Chevy was brand new. Why settle for anything less? So what if we were without a stick of furniture?

Kings Highway Blvd. and Avenue O was not far from famed Coney Island, about a half hour drive to Kings County Hospital. Only a block away stood a bakery and a beauty shop. It was a wide street with a divider down the middle. From one side rose a large, four story red brick building. Never mind that the stark, unimaginative architecture had all the appeal of a factory. Tiny shrubs and freshly planted trees ringed the outside forecasting happy times ahead. They screamed, "new, new, new." The sign in front said, "One and Two Bedrooms, Available Immediately, see Mgr. in Apt. 201." The reluctant bridegroom tagged along as we rode an elevator to the third floor and inspected a sunny, brightly lit one-bedroom with a Pullman kitchen at one end of the large living room. The bedroom housed a walk-in closet; the bathroom boasted a toilet that had as yet never been flushed! Karl thought I had gone crazy when I leaned over to pull down the shiny handle. The gushing water cut off quickly, as it was supposed to do. "Just checking the plumbing." In truth my mind flashed back to the tobacco stained toilet bowl in that bathroom I had once shared with an old man in a rooming house in New York City when I had run away years before hoping to launch a career as an actress. Now I had narrowly escaped a similar fate in a converted Brooklyn brownstone. We could be happy here, I thought. We would make it our own. It was so fresh, so untarnished, so *new*. I could already picture a new Queen sized mattress against the bedroom wall and a coffee table in front of a grand sofa in the living room. Surely it wouldn't take much to outfit this place, which would bear our stamp. Of course, the rent was twenty dollars a month higher than we had expected to pay, but the good news was that Mr. DeLyra had that day agreed to a full refund.

It had been many years since I sat on my Daddy's lap with a *pretty puleeze*. It had always worked before and I saw no reason why it shouldn't work now.

"Please, Daddy, could you just loan us enough for the security deposit and a mattress? The apartment is so shiny and new. We'd pay it back as soon as I get a job." A no-brainer. I knew Daddy wouldn't be able to resist the magic words, *brand new*.

"Sure, Do. Sign the lease. I'll co-sign and send you a check for whatever you need." My mature, ethical husband agreed but only with the proviso that this was a loan rather than a gift. That was OK with me since I was confident my Dad would not be in a hurry to be repaid.

We returned on Sunday, check in hand. As is the custom in Brooklyn, several matrons were gathered on folding chairs just outside the entrance. I had not yet become accustomed to this habit, one that had never found its way to the South Side of Chicago. We nicknamed them the Chorus of Jewish Trojan Women. Speaking to anyone walking by was their rightful entitlement.

"You taking the one bedroom, or the two?

"Oh? A doctor you're going to be?

"Don't rent on the ground floor—too noisy."

"Sadie, what business is it of yours? The ground floor is less. Maybe they couldn't afford higher." This comes from the mouth of Mrs. Doyle, whom I later learn is the token Irish housewife of the group. As a longstanding Brooklyn resident, her speech is undistinguishable from her Jewish neighbors.

On cue, to the rescue up walks an attractive young couple wheeling a pudgy infant in a shiny oversized blue carriage. "Hi, we're the Coopermans. Alvin and Evelyn. Come on, ride up the elevator with us and we'll show you our two bedroom on the fourth floor." Memories of St. Louis and my penchant for antiques acquired during my time there, fly out the window when I behold the Cooperman apartment, which is furnished with the *au courant* clean lines of leather, chrome and teak wood. I gush to Evelyn that I love what she has done with the place. Alvin advises us that he works in Manhattan, not a bad commute from here. "Karl's going to be an intern at Kings County Hospital" I boast, thinking that Alvin, at the very least, must have a job on Wall Street. Evelyn volunteers that her husband is in "entertainment." My attention shifts. I am suddenly, as the saying goes, "all ears." Alvin lets us know that he hopes to produce shows one day but right now he is merely an assistant–assistant to a successful producer by the name of Lee Shubert. It's easy to tell that even Karl is impressed at the mention of the Shubert name, and my insides are already churning. Where did I pack my 8x10 glossies and my resume? If I run down to the Chevy I'm certain I could find one in the trunk. What then? Hand it to Lee Shubert's assistant in hopes that it would lead to a Broadway audition? *Settle down, Mrs. F. Remember your promise outside the Dairy Queen.* So I absorb the news with feigned equanimity and bend down to tickle the Cooperman baby. I am now certain that we were fated to live in this building. Alvin uncorks a bottle of white wine, already toasting his new neighbors. We clink glasses and he tells us that they are preparing to open a new show soon entitled *Guys and Dolls* and perhaps we would like an invitation to the opening. There will be a big party following the performance and we must come as his guests.

There might be no commute to Manhattan for classes or auditions, yet I would make it to Broadway–to the opening night of *Guys and Dolls*.

WORKING IN A FOREIGN LAND

Our neighbors pointed us to Nostrand Avenue where in one morning we were able to order a bed, a desk, and a chair. In the *Sale* section I spotted a wrought-iron table with a glass top and four chairs. The chairs were upholstered in a cheery criss-cross pattern of yellow and green. "It'll look great just opposite the kitchen–make it seem like a real dining room." A table originally meant for a garden would add a certain panache to a room otherwise bogged down by conventional naugahyde and oak. (Little did I realize that it was destined to service three generations of my family.) It was thrilling to shop for my very own furniture and to sign my new name on printed checks. I had taken Karl's last name as a matter of course, though the thought of it on a marquee or even a playbill seemed out of the question. Pushing that thought to the back of my mind, I happily signed one check after another (in my latest affectation–a backhand signature) knowing that Daddy had made a substantial deposit to our account when our furnished "converted brownstone apartment" fell through. Gleefully I add a "Mrs." in front of my name.

The schedule for Karl's general internship was "24 hours on, 24 hours off." During the day on call he was rarely able to catch more than an hour of sleep, so his day off meant driving straight home and collapsing on our new mattress. Like a dutiful wife, I saw to it that my overworked husband had a hot home-cooked dinner when he arrived home every other evening. His three favorites, fried chicken, meat loaf, and chili, became easy-to-rotate staples. Shopping posed a problem at first when I discovered that going to a market in New York meant several different stops—one for meats, another for dairy, a third for produce and finally, one for bakery goods. Then there was something with the sign, *Appetizing.* I had no clue as to what they sold, but it they tout it like that, it must be fresh and delicious. I'd check it out later. Following local custom, I bought a shopping cart on wheels and brazenly began calling the shopkeepers by name. The bakery held a fascinating array of something called "danish" which resembled the sweet rolls I had grown up with in Chicago. The one that attracted my attention was golden brown, sprinkled with sliced almonds with five tiny ovals on one end. I worked up the courage to point them out to the harried sales clerk as she sliced my challah, "Rosie, what are those sweet rolls called?"

"What do you mean, sweet rolls? What's a sweet roll? Those are Danish. Those are *beah clawrs.*"

"Baaclors? What's in them?"

"Not baaclors! Beah clawrs! They're filled with almond paste."

That night I surprised Karl with the gooey pastry and proudly announced their name. Evelyn Cooperman had come down from the fourth floor to borrow a tea bag. I invited her to join us for dessert. Fortunately for me, Evelyn had spent time in the mid-west. "Dottie, those are bear claws! See the little toes? Bear claws!" Certainly Brooklyn had its own customs, but I hadn't counted on having to master a different language. Years of elocution lessons in Chicago had of course included "Voice and Diction" which I smugly perceived to have mastered. The importance of a broad A and a hard R were emphasized in my hometown. It would be years before I was able to let go of them.

The furniture arrived. Just as I had envisioned, the glass top wrought iron table not only looked charming but was a perfect fit. Sparse as it was, the remainder of the large living room had a pleasant, comfortable feel. Finishing touches could wait until our coffers were replenished.

The trousseau towels were folded and hung on the shiny chrome bars. "His" and "Hers" toothbrushes rested side by side in a large shaving mug, with no thought of sharing it with others. There was little more that required my attention. Time for me to go to work. The Brooklyn Eagle was opened again to the want ads, but this time to the "Help Wanted" columns.

"Secretary, shorthand required, Nurse, Travel Agent, Welder." Welder? My BA in English Lit. qualified me for nothing that could earn a living in the real world. Just a minute: "Receptionist and Dental Assistant. Immediate opening. Will train." Sure, I could do that. The address was only a block away.

A.A. Goldberg, DDS must have been the kindest, warmest, funniest, most patient, Brooklyn boy ever to complete dental school. His assistant had left suddenly and could I start right away? Maybe the next day?

"Sure, but why not today? My husband is on call; he won't be home until morning. I don't even have to fix dinner."

No need to negotiate the salary. I was hired! What a thrilling new experience to be so eagerly accepted without so much as an audition.

"Dr. Goldberg's office. One moment please. Dr. Goldberg's office. Hold please. Sorry, now how may I help you?" Though I had never before used a telephone with two lines, it took me only a few minutes to nearly master the push button system. "Oh, sorry. Did I disconnect you? I thought I had you on hold. What was that name again? *Howaad*? How do you spell that? H-O-W-A-R-D? Oh, your mean *Howard*." Correct English pronunciation had definitely not spread to Brooklyn. My voice had a pleasant sound and an air of professionalism that I was certain far surpassed that of the former receptionist. Despite the language barrier this was a cinch. I couldn't wait to tell Karl.

By the following morning I have answered calls, made appointments, canceled appointments, mastered the filing system, and have everything running smoothly. The calls taper off. Perhaps I will be able to get in some reading between rings. Dr. Goldberg motions for me to step into his office where a patient is reclining with her mouth wide open. He picks up a drill and goes to work on what I later learn to be her second molar. It appears that Dr. Goldberg expects me by his side whenever he peers into an open mouth. The issue that he had glossed over lightly was that the "receptionist" part of the job was inconsequential. One week later I am accustomed to his orders: "Swab, please, mix a double amalgam filling please. Take a set of bite wing x-rays and develop them right away please." By the second week I am a step ahead of him and already a whiz at preparing fillings and developing x-rays. A bigger challenge would present itself a few days later when A.A. suddenly asked me to hand him a *guttapucha*. A *guttapucha?* I'm sorry Dr. Goldberg, but I don't know where we keep the *guttapuchas*. "It's that long sharp instrument. Here it is right here. See? A guttapucha." The light bulb goes on. He is speaking Brooklynese, of course. He is asking for his "gutter percher" which was in a drawer clearly marked. "Receptionist" had a hint of glamour and was a role I could willingly play. "Dental Assistant" was another matter, but it was the one that would earn me my paycheck. Memorizing names of dental instruments and molars was a far cry from memorizing lines, but I could handle it for now.

If Dr. Goldberg had omitted details of the job, he couldn't be faulted, for I also had omitted a detail of my own. In less than eight months I would be leaving this or any other job, for, as I suspected, I was already pregnant.

FIRSTBORN

The Birthing

"Let's call it August 1ˢᵗ" said my friendly OB/Gyn when I nagged him for a "due date." August 1ˢᵗ. A good round number. So my baby would be a Leo. But perhaps not. After all, since this pregnancy had come as a surprise, perhaps the doctor miscalculated. I felt fairly certain that I would deliver by the end of July. Of course the baby could come early, perhaps as early as mid July. Just in case, I'd better study up on the zodiac sign of "Cancer." I penciled August 1ˢᵗ in my calendar, but only very, very lightly. I really didn't believe in astrology, but it was fun. I knew several Leos. As Lions they were leaders rather than followers. Positive thinkers. A good sign. As for Cancers, or Crabs, they were even more interesting: true romantics, compassionate and contradictory, eccentric and sensitive both. I'd aim for a July date, despite Dr. Sohgar's prediction.

In early spring I sprung the news on Dr. Goldberg. By now I was certain that my pregnancy was so obvious, that I'd better purchase some of the maternity smocks that were in fashion for expectant mothers. I offered to continue working as long as he'd have me. No problem, he said, but perhaps I should be extra careful when developing the x-rays. Scientists were bandying about a theory that exposure to radiation could harm a fetus. As, perhaps, could alcohol. As, perhaps, could cigarettes. I had already given up smoking, but was an outstanding martini-mixer and saw no reason to abandon Karl in our nightly cocktail ritual.

By the end of June I had quit work and was suffering both the New York humidity and nightly leg cramps. *Come on, Baby, let's get this over with.*

It never even occurred to me that I would have to endure pregnancy for more than the prescribed nine months! But Baby had its own agenda. The sign of Cancer came and went. Although my brown luggage set had included an "overnight case" it just wouldn't do for this event. Finding just the right case was worth a subway trip to Wanamaker's. There I bought the perfect, cheerful, flowered little suitcase which I carefully filled with all the essentials that were listed in my pregnancy manual, including a lovely mauve bed jacket with a ribbon at its neck. Perfect for nursing my baby and receiving visitors at the same time.

Summer was here, which meant the stoop brigade was out in full force. Since there was but one entrance to our apartment I was forced to pass them when coming or going.

"So when are you due?"

"So how are you feeling?"

"Looks like you've dropped."

"Nu. You're still here?"

"Leave her alone already, Sadie. Can't you see she's still here?"

"She's late."

Yes, I am late, but leave me alone already. What could I do about it other than make my poor husband miserable, as though he was somehow responsible. August 1st. came and went. My little well-packed suitcase waited patiently at the front door like a soldier awaiting orders to do battle.

August 10th! Surely the baby must want to be born by now. By dinner that night I was feeling slight stomach cramps. We called Obstetrics. Come in if you really feel you might be dilating they told me.

"Karl. I really am having pains. I think we should take my suitcase and go." Karl pulls the blue Chevy to the front of the building, waiting while I pass the chorus. All eyes are on me as I stride to the car, but perhaps from a sense of decency, they are strangely quiet eyeing me with a kind of reverence as I pass.

"False Labor" comes the cheery diagnosis at Kings County. "You can go home now."

"Well well, look who's here! She's back already."

"Now, Ladies. Hold your tongue. When her baby's ready to be born, it'll be born."

Bless sweet Mrs. Mary-Margaret Doyle from the first floor."

I manage a smile, hold my head high as I disappear into the elevator.

The following day my less than eager obstetrician assured me a due date was not an exact science but agreed to "induce labor" if It did not soon begin on its own. The very term had a ring of horror. Not only unnatural but painful as well, I had been warned. Nonetheless, I fell into a sound sleep, only to be jolted awake at midnight. This was it. No doubt about it. How could I have mistaken those puny little stomach cramps for the real thing? With Karl's arm around me, we hurried to the Chevy. The guardians of the stoop had long since pulled in their tents.

Because he was a staff doctor, Karl was awarded the privilege of remaining with me throughout the entire ordeal. After six hours he was wishing he had become an engineer. Finally he himself was urging the nurses to summon the doctor. Large doses of demerol and scopolamine had me hallucinating in between contractions. Over and over I ordered Karl to "pick that banana up off the floor!" My rotund, kindly old OB/Gyn finally arrived, smiling as he pulled on his rubber gloves. "She's ready. Let's go. Needle please."

A prick to my lower back and pure bliss. No more pain. Blessed, blessed spinal block. I could still push, but now I did so with a smile on my face. 9:21 a.m. "It's a girl"

* * *

Baby Naming

She was to be named for Karl's Aunt Jean, who had died the year before. Jean's sister, Aunt Millie, campaigned for the name Jennifer, which had recently come into fashion, but I hated the idea of a "Jennie," because it had been my grandmother's outdated name. Shakespeare's *Merchant of Venice* was a favorite of mine and I always admired Shylock's gutsy daughter, Jessica. The only other *Jessicas* known at the time were the actress Jessica Tandy and the opera star Jessica Dragonette. "Jessie" seemed like a good nickname. So "Jessica" it was. The nurse who filled out the birth certificate had no idea how to either pronounce or spell it. Nor did many of our friends or neighbors, who thought it rather cruel to saddle a little girl with such a moniker. Aunt Millie never forgave us. Many years later, as the name climbed to the top of the charts, I thought of apologizing to my daughter for my lack of imagination. For the first time in my life, the wrong time, I had become a trend setter.

*   *   *

Postpartum Ups & Downs

The maternity ward of Kings County Hospital was hardly the place for the rich and famous. The hospital was just what the name implied: a County hospital catering to those of limited means. The maternity ward was comprised of three long rooms with beds laid side by side a foot or two apart, similar to the wards we are used to seeing for injured soldiers. A few private rooms were set aside for wives of the medical staff so I was one of the chosen few. No sooner was Jessica born than I was whisked into number 401. The decor left much to be desired. The walls were an olive drab paint, badly in need of a fresh coat; the bed was standard hospital issue, as were the linens. The biggest plus was that a private bathroom was within feet of my bed. I was to remain in the hospital five days, standard practice in 1951.

My pediatrician was aghast when he heard I was determined to breast feed. "Why put yourself through that when there are so many wonderful new products on the market? You will be less stressed and your baby will be just as healthy with a bottle filled with formula."

When the nurses realized I was adamant, they brought little Jessica to me every four hours and I propped myself up on two or three pillows in an attempt to nurse her. Karl came by with our box camera to capture the moment.

By the second day I felt well enough to walk myself the few steps to the bathroom. In the middle of the night I got up to relieve my bladder, but as I turned on the lavatory light I was seized by a pain in my head, a pain like no other. I managed to stumble back into bed but just barely. A knife began at the top of my scalp and shot through my neck and shoulder blades all the way down my back. This was no ordinary headache. I rang for the nurse who clucked sympathetically and brought me an aspirin. It didn't help. I lay awake the remainder of the night attempting a diagnosis as the knife continued to shoot down my spine. Polio was still in epidemic stage and from everything I remembered, a painful neck was a major symptom. Or perhaps it was a brain tumor. At best I would spend the rest of my life in an iron lung, at worst, I would not live long enough to bring my new baby home. What rotten luck! Just as my life was beginning. How and why did this happen to me at what was meant to be the happiest time of my life? When Karl arrived early the next morning before starting his rounds he found me in tears. I expected him to spring into action, immediately notifying a specialist. Instead he gave me a kiss on the cheek and ordered a sleeping pill so I could get some rest. This was unacceptable behavior from my knight in shining armor. How could he be so cavalier about my misery, my serious symptoms? I covered my face with my hands, shutting my eyes tight and bit down hard, grinding my teeth as I had so often been warned against doing.

When my obstetrician arrived that afternoon for his daily round the headache had subsided somewhat and he seemed not too concerned. That evening it was back full force. The pediatrician arrived the following morning to supervise the breast feeding regimen. When I told him of the unbearable pain, he suggested stopping the nursing. Out of the question! Again I raised my head on the pillows to assist my suckling infant. The pain returned full blast. While little Jessie was taken for a play date with her peers in the nursery I was beginning to doze when the door to my private room burst open and like a gust of wind, a panama hat, a rumpled seersucker suit, a walking stick, and a handsome six-foot stranger blew in.

"Hi, Dee! Just came from the nursery an' I knew right off which one was yours. You got de cutest little white baby I ever did see."

This was no stranger. This was the former love of my life, Jay Irving Landesman. My head was throbbing with the worst pain my body had ever known, yet I laughed as only Jay could make me laugh. My heart began to race. I knew Jay was living in New York, but what was he doing here? How did he even know about the baby and where I was? Oh, God, I must look awful. I didn't want him to see me this way. Not only was my hair a mess, I wore no makeup, but worst of all, I wasn't up to the snappy comeback or the delicious repartee that he and I always expected of one another. I raised my achy arm to smooth down my bangs, and at that moment I knew. I knew even though back at the Dairy Queen in Ohio when I had sworn to Karl that the theatre was "out of my system," that Jay was still very much in it. And would be for a long, long time.

The next morning Jessie-baby was in my arms as I propped myself in my usual breast-feeding position.

"Good Morning, Mrs. Friedman. What a beautiful baby! My name's Dr. Auerbach and I'm the intern on Maternity today. How are you feeling?"

"Hi, Doctor Auerbach. Well, to tell you the truth, this hasn't been the happy experience I was expecting."

His manner was upbeat and friendly, his smile warm, inviting me to pour out my saga. Before I was finished with the excruciating detail, he interrupted: "You said you were given an epidural, right? Well, didn't anyone tell you to keep your head down for at least the first twenty-four hours?"

Head down? Well, no. I had elevated my head to breast feed and had gotten up and walked shortly after I left the delivery room.

"But Dorothy. You had what's known as a *caudal headache*. Many patients get them after a spinal injection, that's why we are warned to keep them lying flat for at least 24 hours. But not to worry; they go away. Keep your head down and by the time you leave you'll be just fine."

I'm going to leave the hospital and go home with my baby? No iron lung? No brain surgery?

"How come no one told me?"

"Well, it's like this. Some medics believe it's all psychological and that just putting the idea in the patient's head will bring it on. Then, too, if you were on the ward with other patients, the pain seems to spread like wildfire the moment one patient complains. We're taught not to discuss this, so please don't mention that I told you—not to your husband or your OB/Gyn. I'm glad I could make you feel better; have a wonderful life with your beautiful daughter."

And he was off. Gone, but never to be forgotten.

I *did* mention it to Karl, of course. His response was that same knowing smile that later became known to me as "Psychiatrist's Smug." Did he ever believe me my pain was real? I would never be certain.

NEW MOMMY

Mrs. Bortz

I made certain to keep my head down until the signal to take my precious baby home. A wheelchair was brought to my room and, just like in the movies, my doctor-husband led me to our car as I held tight to the little pink swaddled bundle in one arm, the plant that Aunt Flo and Uncle Eddie had sent in the other. To my delight, a warm sunny morning had brought the Greek Chorus out in full force. No wishing to sneak past them this time. My status had changed forever: I was now officially anointed a Mom.

"How long were you in labor?"

"How much did she weigh?"

"So give us a peek already."

"She looks exactly like my Gloria looked."

And finally: "What's her name?"

Jessica? Jessica? What kind of a name is that? How do you spell it? Nobody will ever remember it.

As in the past, Mary-Margaret Doyle came to my rescue. "It's a perfectly beautiful name. Now girls, let the new mommy get her baby upstairs. Congratulations, you two."

I flashed Mrs. Doyle a grateful smile as we hurried to the elevator and up to the third floor to exchange the cheering section for the sanctuary of our own private love nest. A quiet lie-down on our new mattress with an infant snuggled contentedly between Mommy and Daddy was the black and white photo flashing through my head.

The door flings open before Karl's keys are out.

"Velcome! Velcome! I haf been vaiting for you. Here, let me take her."

My arm tightens around my seven pound bundle. Was I never to be free of mother-figures? In my eagerness to get home I had forgotten all about Sonia Bortz, the infant nurse that we had hired for the first two weeks of Jessie's life. There she stood, all five feet of her, a take-charge bundle of energy. Common wisdom held that no new mommy should be expected to do without an infant nurse. My parents were picking up the tab. Mrs. Bortz had come highly recommended and in the one interview we had with her she seemed pleasant and certainly capable. A woman in her seventies, her accent was a mystery, even to me, a self-styled dialect expert. Czech? Austrian? Hungarian? No matter. Although a nap did seem like a good idea, I am not prepared to relinquish control.

Jessica, who had slept soundly all the way home let out a loud wail at the very touch of this stranger, as though she understood who was number one in this scenario.

"She's hungry. You lie down. I'll prepare ze formula and give her a bottle." Bottle? Was there a language barrier at play? Hadn't the woman heard me or understood me at our interview?

"No, no, Mrs. Bortz. We discussed that. Remember? She's being breast-fed. No bottle. No formula. I'll just take her into the bedroom and feed her."

A look of horror crossed over Sonia Bortz' face. "Yes, yes, you said zat. But she's hungry. She needs more milk. I'll just give her one bottle while you take a nap."

Thus began the Battle of the Bottle. My obstetrician and pediatrician both had disapproved of breast feeding, stopping just short of making it a command. It was the 'fifties–the age of the bottle baby, with a new formula being introduced every other week. "Wean your baby, liberate yourself!" was the cry of the day.

Sonia Bortz worked only a six-day week, but each of those days meant she was on call 24 hours. While her charge slept she intended to fold diapers, sterilize bottles, and prepare the next batch of *Similac*. At the first cry she was would be ready to test the temperature of the milk from the stream of the rubber nipple as she jiggled the hungry baby in the crook of one arm. Next she could settle down to a nice long session of guzzling, interrupted only by an occasional over-the-shoulder burp. By nursing my baby not only would I rob her of her customary routine, I would deprive her of her *raison d'être*. To fill in some of her leisure time, Mrs. Bortz began to cook. To Karl's delight our little apartment was filled with overpowering odors of sauerbraten, liver and onions, and beef stroganoff.

My master plan was to prove that a breast fed baby would be happier, healthier, more content, but Jessica stubbornly refused to cooperate. Although she loved her feedings, they never seemed to be sufficient for long. Rather then settling into a contented sleep, she would continue to fuss, her pretty little lips repeating their sucking motion. Mrs. Bortz, who never left our side, came up with a theory: "Maybe your milk isn't reech enough" she would insist, eyeing the cans of supplements lined up on the shelf above the kitchen sink like soldiers awaiting their orders.

As the first week drew to a close I felt as if I was really losing it. Not only did I have no privacy and very little rest, I had a daughter who seemed to look at me accusingly, corroborating her nurse's diagnosis. Raising my voice at Mrs. Bortz would release some tension, but I forced myself to hold in my infamous temper. The rare times Karl came home he rocked the baby, sung to her, then handed her to her infant nurse while his crabby wife caught a few winks. If I thought I would get support from him I was sadly mistaken. "Do, have some empathy. The poor woman is just trying to do her job. Don't push it–we don't want to lose her."

The last straw! Even my husband was taking the side of a stranger against mine. This might be enough to push me into a full blown postpartum depression. I must change my approach. I would try humor. The next day I began joking with her, teasing her about her accent, but her European sensibility did not respond. Ready to explode with a need to talk this out I knew what I had to do.

"I'm so sorry, Mrs. Bortz, but we're all out of Kellogg's Corn Flakes. Do you mind terribly going down to Waldbaum's while the baby is asleep? I'll be fine"

A reluctant Mrs. Bortz hurried to the grocery store. I dialed Aunt Flo the moment the door shut behind her.

I poured my heart out as I always could with Flo. "Maybe I'm wrong to be so stubborn. Maybe I should just give in and let her give the baby a bottle. Maybe I should just let her win."

Giving in was not part of Aunt Flo's DNA.

"What are you talking about, Kiddo? This is *your* baby. Who's the boss? If she doesn't like it she can lump it. What's the worst thing that can happen? She'll walk out? Doe, remember how you helped out when Genie was a tiny baby and I had to go to work? You don't need her. You can take care of Jessica yourself. Just sleep whenever you can catch a nap and don't worry about cooking or housework."

"But Flo, Karl will kill me if she leaves."

"If Karl gets angry, believe me, he'll get over it. Hold your ground, but try sweet-talking her first. Don't lose your temper. Remember the old saying–*you can catch more flies with honey.*"

There it was. So simple, as only Flo could put it.

When Sonia returned from the market (with Bran Flakes) I graciously thanked her and then sat her down for our first real heart-to-heart. This time my tone was decidedly sugar coated. I opened my bible—Dr.

Spock's *Infant and Child Care* to the pages wherein he extols the virtues of breast feeding, hoping it might help her understand why I wanted so much to give my daughter a good start in life. I took her hand in mine, telling her how anxious I was to be her friend for the remainder of our time together. Suddenly I was back in the Little Theatre at the University of Wisconsin in my class, *Scene Study for Seniors, 3 units*. I was Nora pleading with Torvald to believe in my love. I looked deeply into Sonia Bortz' eyes, and for the first time I felt her melting. She promised she'd try to be open minded, and in return I promised that she could teach me how to bathe Jessica. As an added bonus I said she could dress the baby in a tiny checked gingham outfit the next day when my cousin Betty came to visit from Forest Hills.

The first bath gave Mrs. Bortz a new lease on life. She was positively euphoric as she gently scrubbed Jess's belly button and showed me how to gently wash her silky brown hair. I had been looking forward to experiencing this milestone together with Karl, but hey, wasn't I used to compromising?

Finally, the two-week stint was up. We had made it! The baby nurse hugged me as she picked up her little brown suitcase, but I could swear she breathed a sigh of relief as she departed for her next job, hopefully with a new mommy who would be all too happy to put her in full charge of feedings. I doubt I had convinced her of the value of mother's milk, but I did manage to memorize her recipe for beef stroganoff, which would eventually become my signature dish.

Stage Mommy

To Whom It May Concern:

Attached please find two snapshots of my infant daughter, Jessica Rae. I believe you will agree that Jessica is a perfect "Gerber Baby" and as such would be a marvelous replacement for the model presently being used on Gerber baby food jars. At the very least, she belongs in your print ads. I can be contacted at _____

After the departure of Mrs. Bortz Jessica was all mine, which meant I now had the pleasure of feeding, burping, and diapering her 24/7.

Thankfully, we could afford a diaper service which picked up the dirties three times a week, replacing them with freshly laundered folded ones. Not as easy as the ads proclaimed, we were expected to rinse the soiled ones before tossing them into the laundry bag. In short order, my back rebelled with a nagging dull pain from bending over a very low toilet for what seemed like every hour on the hour. Even though breast-feeding precluded the laborious task of sterilizing bottles, it brought with it other travails including blocked ducts and sore nipples.

We soon discovered that our Jessie had her own very rigid ideas of what was known as a "schedule." Her plan was to turn night into day, sleeping soundly while the sun shone, eating, drinking, pooping, and occasionally cooing as soon as night fell. My bio-rhythm stubbornly clung to its old ways. Within a month or so I was a complete wreck. Karl seemed to be on one rotation after another that demanded him remaining on call at the hospital all night. Was he faking it, choosing a skimpy cot over our queen-sized mattress, merely for the sake of an uninterrupted five or six hours? I couldn't be certain, but deep inside I had to admit that, given a choice, I might have opted for the same.

On rare occasions a visitor from Manhattan would arrive with a squeaky stuffed animal or a pair of pink booties for a look at the much heralded new arrival. I couldn't wait. For the one thing I knew for sure, awake or asleep, was that Jessica was beautiful, in fact, she had to be one of the most beautiful babies ever born. Karl's genes and mine had somehow combined to produce a perfect specimen and I couldn't wait to show her off. Unhappily, she had other ideas. The moment the doorbell would ring; she went into "Do Not Disturb" mode, falling into a deep slumber that I longed for her to replicate after sundown. Tickling her did no good, nor did jiggling or banging pots and pans, a noise that ordinarily sent her into paroxysms and screams. The arrival of a guest sent a clear signal that it was nap-time. Lids would clamp tight, obliterating her best feature—a pair of gorgeous large round brown eyes with unbelievably long lashes.

Not to be outdone by the Coopermans, we had purchased an enormous blue and steel grey baby carriage on Nostrand Avenue. During the day the contraption stood near the elevator as was accepted custom, but at night it was wheeled into our tiny foyer, a ready-made firetrap blocking any possibility of an emergency exit. Finally it was time for Jessica's debut. I tied the ribbon of a bonnet under chin and wheeled her out for her grand entrance. It was a sunny day; the reception committee was out *en masse*. The double doors swung open and it was all I could do to avoid taking a bow. They relinquished their folding chairs to gather round the buggy.

Kootchi, kootchi, koo. chirped 4-B as she gave the baby a little pinch on the cheek.

A-boo! spat out Mrs. Greenblatt from 2-C. Jessie obliged with a long burp followed by a little mother's milk escaping from her gorgeous lips. It trickled down her tiny bib on which were embroidered the words, *Grandpa's Favorite*.

The roar of laughter that followed might have offended me, had not Jessica chosen that moment to break out in a what could be interpreted as huge smile. Everyone burst into applause, even the crabby Mrs. Mendel who lived one floor beneath us and had already complained that she could hear my footsteps in the middle of the night as I rushed to comfort my crying baby. These women were my friends. I loved them all. Why had I resented them during those long months of my summer pregnancy? Couldn't I tell that they appreciated me, that I was like a daughter to them?

"Oh, Dorothy, she is just adorable. Just too cute for words."

"She should be in the movies."

"If not in the movies, at least in a magazine" Mrs. Doyle contradicted.

"What do you mean a magazine? Her picture should be on the jars of baby food– you know, like that Gerber Baby."

Modest now, I demurred. "Oh, no, no. She's no prettier than Linda Tanenbaum next door." Linda Tanenbaum indeed! That overweight little butterball without a hair on her head! "Well, see you later, we're going to take a little walk."

By the time we reached the corner of Avenue Q, my imagination had taken full flight. My heart was doing somersaults. Karl would be home for dinner that night. We must get out the camera. I will walk down to the drug store now for a fresh supply of flash bulbs. We must keep Jess awake long enough for some good photos. A baby this beautiful belonged on the front of an applesauce jar. Of course, it might mean going into Manhattan several times a week to meet with agents and eventually to photo shoots. But I was ready. I could do that. It wasn't actually acting. It was just a photograph. And it wasn't for me, but for our child. And it paid big money. And we could put it away towards her college education. And it wasn't as if this was actually the *theatre*. Was it?

THE DYE IS CAST

Karl is now a bona-fide doctor on the staff of a famed sanatorium where he is a resident pulmonologist. I am reading Tolstoy on the manicured, hilly lawn while my expanding family of beautiful babies plays nearby. We live rent free on the beautiful estate where through our bedroom window, we have an unobstructed view of the lovely Swiss Alps. We have just finished our afternoon ritual of hot chocolate and mouth watering pastries—apple strudel, macaroons, palmiers, and the children's favorite: cream puffs. Three days a week with those patients well enough to partake I hold play readings, followed by stimulating discussions. I have almost mastered French and my accent is such that I could be mistaken for a native. On weekends we join the brilliant medical staff for opulent dinners after which there is brandy and talk sprinkled with gayety and laughter. No subject is off-limits, from the relation between time and space to the latest theories of Sigmund Freud. One of the younger doctors clearly has eyes for me. At his request, I follow him into the library for a series of delicious stolen kisses. They are a mere distraction with little meaning, for I am still in love with my sexy husband. Karl is on the brink of discovering a cure for tuberculosis, which will insure his place in medical annals.

On this rare lazy afternoon I have permitted myself the luxury of indulging in one of my favorite pastimes, aka, the "daydream." Jessica is bathed and sound asleep after a contented feeding in my arms. I am expecting my husband-the-intern shortly for a dinner that is warming in the oven. I doze off again.

Now Karl is at a sleek podium receiving his Nobel Prize. Flashbulbs pop all around us. The room is alive with the very same paparazzi that cover the Oscars, the Emmys and the Tonys. A microphone is shoved into my face:

"How does it feel to be married to a famous scientist, Mrs. Friedman? They say there's a woman behind every successful man. Is that true in your case?" Not wishing to detract from my husband's moment of glory, I gaze up at his five feet, ten inches, and respond demurely, "You'll have to ask him."

Karl was now midway into his general internship at Kings County, which meant the time had come for him to choose a specialty. This is tantamount to a college student declaring a major if not more daunting. Unless your ambition was limited to that of a general practitioner somewhere on rural plains, it was wise to continue training so as to become Board Certified as a specialist. The payoff for several more lean and grueling years meant more prestige and a fatter wallet. In Karl's case, I thought that choosing a specialty would be a no-brainer. His mother, Mary, had suffered from a severe case of tuberculosis since shortly after his birth. She had spent several years in a TB sanatorium before her early death. In his late 'teens Karl himself had contracted the disease and was sent to a similar facility where after a year or so he was deemed well enough to serve in the army. Admitted to medical school on the GI Bill after his discharge, there was little doubt in his mind that he would spend his professional life treating this debilitating disease. Pulmonary medicine would be his fate. But fate itself has a habit of intervening, and before his internship was completed, research had moved so quickly that TB had all but become a thing of the past. Now our future had become a question mark.

I had rarely seen Karl excited on any of his rotations. Delivering babies held little appeal, nor did treating them later as a pediatrician. His aversion to blood plus his rather advanced age disqualified him for a career as a surgeon. Oncology was too depressing. While on duty in the department of dermatology, however, he seemed to come alive, often outdistancing his fellow interns in the diagnosis of skin problems. And hadn't he cleared up Jessie's diaper rash in record time? Dermatology almost never required emergency night calls, which to my sleep-deprived husband appeared to be the deal breaker. So I managed to conjure up only the slightest degree of suspense when Karl telephoned to say that he had reached a decision. The dye was cast, I thought. I would become Mrs. Doctor Acne. Time for one more daydream, another wherein I find fulfillment in the reflected glory of My Man.

It was a matter of only a short time before Karl would be promoted to Chief of Staff of the hospital of his choice. As the wife of this prestigious man, I would be awarded full use of the grounds and the facilities, which were spacious enough to rehearse and perform in-house productions of The Matchmaker *and* My Sister Eileen. *"Doctor's wife spurns offers of Broadway," read the headlines in the Daily Star, just under my photo in costume as Dolly Levi. "Says she is staying put in her role as doctor's wife–of greater use as star and director of plays that bring joy to the serious and terminally ill."*

Karl leaves the hospital early enough to make an unprecedented stop for a bouquet of flowers. He brings them into the bedroom where I still doze in a state of bliss. He stands at the foot of the bed and looks down.

"OK, Do. I've made my decision. I told them today at the hospital so we can begin planning our next move."

"You've made up your mind without discussing it with me? O.K. Honey, so what's it going to be?"

"This may come as a surprise, but I've decided to do a residency in psychiatry."

He's kidding, of course. I look up for a smile or a smirk–anything to assure me that he is not serious. But, no, rarely have I seen a more determined expression on his face. Psychiatry? Psych*iatry*? Karl? Karl whose Marxist political views demanded that he dismiss this new specialty as pure hokum! Karl, who ridiculed impressionable fellow interns already intrigued by it. Karl, who never wanted to hear about my psychoanalysis, who felt the study of medicine unnecessary to deal with neurotics. *That* Karl? That Karl now stands before me expecting an endorsement of his choice. I realize he is waiting for an enthusiastic response but it would be hypocritical to play along without raising an objection. Here he is, still in his scrubs, a stethoscope around his neck, a drop of blood splattered on his pocket, exactly like the drop so romantically displayed on the night he had first been introduced to my parents. Karl had so much to offer as a doctor of internal medicine; he was so brilliant, he was so adept at math and at science, but so often lacking in the personal skills that I knew first hand to be key to a successful psychiatric practice. Was he about to trade in that stethoscope for a pad of paper and a pen as he sat cross-legged on a leather Herman Miller chair, glancing at the clock, hoping the hands would move faster until the hour was up? This was the man I had met at a fund-raising party for a left wing political group, the man I had fallen in love with. His political beliefs were in direct conflict with the bourgeois practice of psychotherapy, which was deemed to be of no value to the masses. Karl still remained friends with several interesting Comrades from those days and from his life as a labor organizer. Might this spell the end of those valued relationships?

Worse still, a psychiatrist's personal life is a deeply guarded secret. A picture of my own analyst's family existed nowhere other than in my imagination. Not only would there be no flashbulbs, no newspaper quotes, but his office would boast not one single photo of his wife and kids. So much for glory–reflected or otherwise.

I didn't attempt a smile. "You can't be serious."

But he was.

Arrival in Brooklyn with Statue
of Liberty in background.

New bed in new apartment.

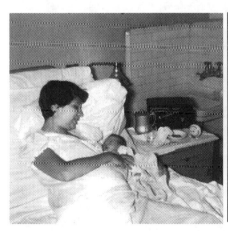

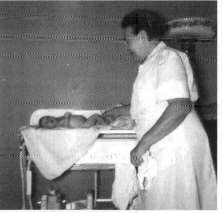

Jessica's first feeding, Kings
County Hospital

Jessica's first bath, Mrs. Bortz.
Kings Highway apartment

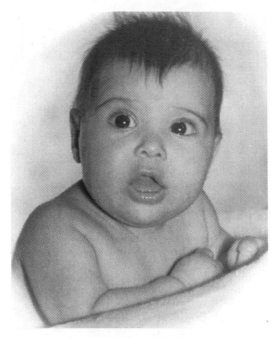

"Gerber Baby"

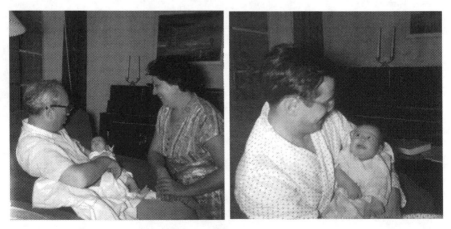

First visit, Grandma Lillian & Grandpa David
with baby Jessica

PART THREE:

ON THE ROAD (AGAIN)

CHICAGO REVISITED

Again the blue Chevy sedan is packed. This time it is headed from east to west and this time it is overloaded not merely with household items but diapers and pacifiers. Jessica is strapped into a cumbersome car bed that takes nearly all the space in the smallish back seat. Not yet one year old she is taking her first cross-country trip, relocating from Brooklyn to Southern California. Common wisdom has it that the motion of a car lulls a baby to sleep. This is not the case with our daughter who seems to be sending a clear message that the apartment on Kings Highway suited her just fine. Holding a baby on your lap in this pre-seatbelt era is against the law, so calming my baby requires my constant wiggling around to the rear. This is not so easy for me now, for I am, as the saying goes, "big with child." Yes, Jessie will become a big sister when she is but fourteen months old. Being pregnant has transformed this cross-country trip from a joyride to a nightmare, for along with keeping my baby happy I must now deal with my own heartburn and far too many pit stops.

No, we didn't plan on this happening—it just did. We have mentioned the forbidden "A" word only once, but with Karl looking hard at age forty, it behooves us to accept it with good grace. My mother, however, has other ideas. She had managed to space her two children an acceptable three years apart, so why couldn't I do the same? For so many years I was victim to her rants, her fears that I would never bless her with legitimate grandchildren, it might be expected that she would tolerate this new turn of events with a modicum of joy. Not so. Her only response to our big news was to attack my oversexed husband. "You're a doctor, Karl, how could you let this happen? Didn't you know better?" Now, rather than boasting to her girlfriends, she must keep the unwelcome news of an unexpected pregnancy a dark secret. I'm smack in the middle of another no-win situation. There is just no pleasing this woman!

We are driving over three thousand miles because Karl has accepted a residency in psychiatry in a lovely suburb of Los Angeles called "Compton" *Compton, California:* the alliteration rolls trippingly off my tongue: *Only twenty-five miles from the heart of Beverly Hills,* states the brochure. It must be close to heaven. We have undertaken this journey due to Karl's distaste for the sight of blood. Unable to dissuade him, unable to point him to a residency in dermatology, I gradually began to accept my role, as a Psychiatrist's wife-in-hiding. The choice of location for his next leg of training had involved many late night discussions. For once Karl did not dare make a unilateral decision. His residency might determine where and how we would spend the rest of our lives. The practice of psychiatry as a full time specialty was in its infancy. Psychiatric training was offered at few places in the United States. We had considered and rejected nearly all of them: Florida: too humid. Chicago: obviously out of the question. New York: we were ready for greener pastures. Topeka, Kansas: the famed Menninger Clinic offered a terrific residency but with it the necessity of relocating again when completed. San Francisco: tempting, but too foggy and cold. It became clear that the ideal choice was Los Angeles. We each had a few friends there and I had my uncle Ben and Karl his favorite elderly Aunt Millie. My mother's eldest brother, Ben, was unquestionably the black sheep in her family of six. He had served in World War I but later disgraced the family by falling love with a two hundred pound divorced vaudeville dancer at the Oriental Theatre in downtown Chicago. Among my favorite memories were afternoons in their hotel apartment when Aunt Lily allowed me to rummage through her glamorous wardrobe trunk as she regaled me with stories of her friends and colleagues in the burlesque business, top billing shared between the famous Marx Brothers and to the Red Hot Mama, Sophie Tucker. Ben and Lily now lived in a quasi-Spanish apartment building on Almont Ave. in Beverly Hills. They were the closest things to show business that my family had ever known. Without realizing it at the time, we had selected the state that tips slightly downward on the United States map. It is said that because of this, California is heavily weighted in "loose nuts and bolts." It was settled. We would live just moments away from the motion picture world. Once again I would find myself a mere stone's throw from the world that I had traded for domesticity and diapers.

Our route would include a layover in Chicago where we would put our Pride and Joy on display, and hopefully I would be able to catch a night of uninterrupted sleep. Fantasies of my mother coming to the rescue for the four a.m. feeding quickly vanished when she assured me that her role as grandmother would be confined only to daytime hours. Although we were assigned my brother Alvin's old room at the far end of the apartment I could never feel comfortable sleeping with a man under my parents' roof. Married for nearly two years I had yet to shake the feeling that doing so was committing a mortal sin.

A sit-down *Shabbos* dinner was the setting for the show-and-tell which included both Karl's Chicago family and my own. Baby Jessica was passed from one set of eager arms to another. Unused as she was to this much attention, she began to enjoy it, bestowing both sides of the family with a big smile and even bigger gurgle. Grandma relaxed into her role, though privately she continued to chastise me for my stupidity in conceiving again at breakneck speed. Even my mild mannered Dad kept inquiring, "what was the hurry?" As was expected, Aunt Flo and Uncle Eddie were overjoyed at the prospect of an expanding family. "Good idea, Do," Flo told me out of earshot, "get it over with early so you can go on and live your life." Karl's beautiful sisters arrived with their husbands and kids, laden with extravagant baby gifts. My joy at unwrapping these lavish surprises was tarnished by the tasteless wisecracks about my having "another one in the oven." As usual my timing was off. Husband, baby, it didn't matter. I could never do anything right. In an attempt to push my due date back by a few weeks, I squeezed into my 'fifties maternity smocks which were unsuccessfully designed to camouflage my condition.

Karl agreed to baby sit while I managed a hurried trip downtown for a session with Dr. Greene. Walking through the lobby of 30 North Michigan, riding the elevator to the eighteenth floor I was overwhelmed with unwelcome nostalgia—nostalgia for a single girl with her life ahead of her. Now, instead of looking forward to meeting a date or a friend for a lighthearted drink after the analytic hour I was weighed down with worry about rushing back to my no doubt fretful baby. My slow, pregnant gait repelled me. I remembered the high heels and the tight knit dress I had worn on my last meeting with Greene–the one during which he had given me permission to transfer my feelings from psychoanalyst to husband. The door to the waiting room was heavier to my touch than I had remembered but the sight of the four upright upholstered chairs, now somewhat the worse for wear, comforted me. I pressed the buzzer to the inner sanctum and sat down to enjoy a glossy copy of *Chicago at Night,* hoping Greene would be running late so as to grant me some extra moments of freedom.

No such luck. The door opens and here is my therapist with his same rimless glasses, his same warm smile offering me an outstretched hand. I fleetingly entertain the notion that the handshake might turn into a hug. I settle for a pat on my shoulder.

"Welcome, Dee. Come in, come in. You look wonderful! So glad you were able to find time to get in."

No judgments. No snide remarks. Before I realized it, I was quietly weeping, letting it all hang out. Greene interrupted before the end of the hour.

"The atmosphere in South Shore is toxic for you. The sooner you put two thousand miles between you and your family the better. You and Karl made a smart decision. Go with a light heart. Start your new life knowing you are on the right road." Permission granted.

I had cut all Chicago ties when I married Karl in the small ceremony that excluded any friends. About the only one I still felt close to was my actress pal, Bunny. Bunny had recently married her longtime boyfriend, the actor Richard Lawrence. This was before television when actors either worked on stage or radio. Chicago was the capital of the radio industry, Our union, which later became, AFTRA, was then merely American Federation of Radio Artists, or AFRA. In 1949 Bunny had been crowned AFRA Queen, thus catapulting her career as a gifted voice-over artist. She was in great demand, constantly racing from audition to job to audition. Richard was also busy working in radio. At the moment they had a small apartment in Old Town and felt no rush to start a family. I settled my baby down for a nap, dragged the extension cord on my parents' phone into the bedroom and quietly dialed Bunny's number. As expected. I caught her on the fly.

"Just a quick hello Bun-Bun before we leave for the Coast."

"Gosh, Dee, can't you at least stay until Sunday? Richard and I are having a big brunch for all his buddies at WBBM and the gang from *Stage for Action*. Everyone you know will be here. It's kind of a farewell to Old Town for us. Dick and I just bought a big old Craftsman house right near Lake Michigan in Evanston. We'll move the end of the month."

My mouth watered, but my throat went dry. A big house in Evanston? How could Bunny and Richard, who were always broke, afford such a thing?

"It's a real fixer-upper," Bunny was carrying on, "but you know, I made so much money last year as the spokeswoman on all the *Accent* commercials, our accountant told us we just had to invest in something. Wish you could see it."

Why had I made this call? Bunny would have never known that we had been in Chicago. I was tempted to replace the black receiver in its cradle so that it would appear we had been disconnected. No, thanks, Bunny, I thought. I have no desire for all my old actors' gang to see me looking like a cow. Besides, Karl would be a fish out of water, but he would never agree to my going alone. I remembered teaching my six-year old drama students to always put a smile in their voice. Widening my mouth into a huge grin, I came back with a sincere: "Gosh, Bunny, that sounds great! A house near the lake. I always wanted to live in Evanston."

But Bunny was already telling me that she dare not tie up the line as she was expecting a call on a Tums Commercial that she was up for.

"That's OK, Bunny. Jessica's just waking up so I gotta run. Write me!"

Jessie was whimpering. I caught a whiff. Her diaper needed changing badly. I picked her up and looked at her beautiful little face. A second later I was rewarded with her *googie-gurgling* sound. The pile of folded cloth diapers was close at hand. I plucked off the top one, folding it into a perfect triangle, laid her on the big bed, cleaned her off. Careful with the large pink-tipped diaper pins, all the while singing *Jack and Jill Went Up The Hill,* I watched as her face beamed. We would go out and show off for Grandma and Grandpa. I patted her head on my shoulder, forgetting all about a career in radio and theatre. Almost.

DOWN ON THE FARM

We drive on unfamiliar rocky, dusty, hilly terrain, deep forests on both sides of the road. We have bypassed St. Louis. Instead we are deep into the Ozark Mountains of Missouri, headed to the working farm that Paula and Fred had bought as their summer getaway. Paula has promised plenty of humidity, plenty fresh-picked corn, plenty of martinis, and plenty of laughs. The entire Landesman clan had gathered there to greet us. Karl raised no objection because he had no inkling that my promise made at the Dairy Queen assuring him that I was finished with acting said nothing about a vow to stop lusting after Jay. This will be the first face-to-face encounter between Jay and Karl so naturally I am more than a little nervous. Is this a smart move? Will the Landesmans approve of him? Will he like them? How awful do I look in these maternity clothes? How can I get my frizzy hair to behave?

That I had had a major love affair was no secret to Karl, but I had sworn to him that it was over, kaput, finished. Like the theatre, I convinced myself that my former lover was out of my system. I was ready and eager to settle down to a peaceful, happy life with a "normal" partner. I hadn't seen Jay since last August, when, in rumpled seersucker suit and walking stick, he had paid a surprise visit to the maternity ward the day after I had given birth to Jessica. By now he was married again, this time to the clever debutante Fran Deitsch, and Paula already had given birth to two of her four sons, Rocco and Knight. One look at Jay's smashing, clever wife was enough to assure me there would be no repeat of that night years before when Pat, wife number one, had unwittingly left us alone in their loft. With a baby still sucking at my breast and another kicking in my belly I was certainly no competition for this fresh-faced, stunning blonde.

The original old farmhouse boasted a host of bedrooms with big brass beds and soft down comforters where we could relax without the disapproving gaze of my uptight parents. To my delight and relief, everyone fell in love with Karl's wry, sarcastic sense of humor. He proved much more clever than I at their favorite pastime, Charades. Pulling on one ear, hopping on his leg like a demented chicken, he showed a surprising lack of inhibition. He helped Fred build a tree house for Rocco and Knight, he even joined the boys the night they climbed up to sleep in it. He had passed muster, he was admitted to The Club, which would eventually be known as "Landesmania." Although I still had to catch my breath at the sight of Jay, Karl's handsome face ran a very close second. As I watched them bonding over martinis I was able to relax. Perhaps I had made a good choice after all.

The fun continued as usual. For our second dinner we were treated to slices of the juiciest, pinkest, most delicious watermelon we had ever tasted. "Where was this grown?" We wanted to know. "Right out in the field on our watermelon patch" "Watermelon patch? We walked all around the farm before. Lots of corn, but we didn't see a watermelon patch. What does it look like? Do they grow on trees? On the ground?" "On the ground. In our patch," chimed the brothers in unison. Jay and Fred would manage to awaken the next morning in time to hit the little grocery store a mile down the road, purchase two more melons, race back, place them at the edge of a cornfield, cover them with soil and leaves, in time to point to the "patch" with pride. Karl, being a bit of a country boy himself, caught on at once and was willing to go along with the gag. It was years later that he revealed the truth to this gullible Chicago girl. These grown-up kids would never change. I kicked back and enjoyed some quality time with Paula.

How could I foresee the future–in which the Landesman brothers would reinvent the image of their city by creating the beautiful, lively nightclub, The Crystal Palace, where the likes of Woody Allen, Barbra Streisand, and Lenny Bruce would get their starts. How could I know that Fran Deitsch Landesman would write a song called *Spring Can Really Hang You Up the Most* that would establish her as one of the most revered lyricists of our generation, that she and Jay together would write a smash musical that would run on Broadway, that they would rebuild their lives in London just before The Beatles craze? Certainly I could not envision Paula's firstborn, Rocco, the little towhead scrambling up to his treehouse, as one of Broadway's most powerful producers? Above all, how could I know that Jay and Fran would be the first to literally write the book on free love and coin the phrase, "Open Marriage?" If I had had held a crystal ball, would I have been content to settle for life in a "lovely suburb just 25 miles from the heart of Beverly Hills?" Probably yes. My Dad had made his way from Eastern Europe as a boy of sixteen, working hard every moment to establish himself as a solid, successful businessman. My American born mother was always striving to keep up with him. Except with my Aunt Flo, I could not remember too many lighthearted moments while growing up. The same held true for Karl's childhood. His mother had died before he was ten, leaving his elder sister to raise him while his father, an idealistic country doctor, had worked hard, sometimes delivering babies in exchange for chickens or eggs. Laughter and pranks were not the order of the day as they had been in the Landesman household, with three devilish boys and one older sister constantly teasing their offbeat, wacky, artistic parents. It was with this family that I had first come to the realization that I, too, could be witty and funny. From my very first night in St. Louis I had experienced a feeling of belonging. I was "home."

Always seeking a fresh audience, later in life Jay tried his hand as a book publisher, a novelist, a playwright, and an organic food maven. Although often successful, he never took himself too seriously, content to play Court Jester to the end. He and Fran would remain in their unorthodox marriage for over sixty years. Could I have done the same, if Jay had placed an antique wedding band on my hand years before? Jay titled the first volume of his memoirs, *Rebel Without Applause*. In my soul I knew I was not really a rebel. I longed for the security of a home in a "beautiful suburb." But some things are meant to remain in our systems forever, not unlike a Dybbuk constantly threatening to resurface. So it has been with Jay in mine. There was no email nor texting, but there was "snail mail" and the telephone. No matter how bleak my life may have felt at any given moment, that familiar greeting, "Is that Dee? Dee Sinclair? Jay Land-e-sman here" could always make me smile, for I knew that within the next moment I would be laughing aloud.

Although Karl was more than six degrees of separation from this gang, coming here with him was probably a wise decision that might bring him closer to understanding the real "me."

As we parted everyone urged us to come back soon, or better still, not to leave at all, but rather to settle in St. Louis where, they assured Karl, he would find no dearth of neurotics to treat.

An itchy heat rash had begun to transform little Jessie into a *qvetchie* baby. Unlike the first day, when there was a stampede to hold her, she had suddenly turned into Typhoid Mary. Time to push on!

California, Here We Come.

ROUGE ET NOIR

We have left the farm a day ahead of schedule. Being around Jay and Fran was wearing thin. On and on they carried about their open marriage insisting that the glue that held them together was stronger than mere sexual fidelity. Karl predicted that their marriage was destined to be short-lived. (How stunned he would have been if he could have foreseen the New York Times obit for Jay that would credit much of his long life to his wife and their sixty-two year marriage.) It was a relief to leave the mosquitoes behind to get a head start on our new life in the *beautiful suburb just twenty-five miles from the heart of Beverly Hills.*

Being with only Karl and my baby is relaxing. I release the confining waistline of my maternity pants and breathe a loud, contented sigh. An "open marriage," is just not part of my DNA, nor am I rebel enough to envision a Dionysian whirlwind of a life. The realization, however, does not keep me from fantasizing about St. Louis, about New York, about what might have been. Route 66 finally takes us into Nevada where garish signs relentlessly tout the latest casinos and hotels in Las Vegas–the gambling capital of the world. Since it's but a few miles out of our way, I see no reason why we should not make the detour that could transform our last days of freedom into a memorable event.

Karl's predictable response is an emphatic "no way." If it were Jay, I thought, we'd already be speeding there. Gambling was in the Landesman blood; a detour to the green felt tables would be a given. "Please, Karl, we're one day ahead of schedule, and who knows when we'll ever be able to come back here? I could use a soak in a hot tub in a hotel. Please, Honey." I recognized my old familiar whine. Daddy could never resist my *pretty puleeze* and now I hoped it would have the same effect on my grown-up doctor spouse. Sure enough Karl swerved the wheel to the right. We had made it across the Mojave Desert in the pre-air conditioning days of July, and I suspect he was as anxious as I for a good shower and a cold drink. Getting my way had required but three or four "pulleezes."

Now the road turned to sand, our open windows sucking in their stinging particles like so many pins and needles. Through burning eyes we spotted decrepit filling stations and tiny grocery stores dotting the terrain, each boasting silver slot machines in full view. In between was a seemingly endless stretch of desert, relieved every so often by a clump of incredibly beautiful saguaro cactus plants. To my Midwestern eye, they seem like the eighth wonder. Out comes my Brownie camera for a snapshot. "Pull over, Karl. It'll only take a minute," And, leaving a tiny baby in her car bed, out I hop to capture myself in black and white standing tall beside this majestic, thorny, tree like creature.

Finally the two-lane road gives way to a paved four-lane highway, and the famed Vegas Strip materializes. On our right is a glitzy hotel called the *Tropicana*. Blinking lights outline the figure of a sexy showgirl. A few miles up the road a neon camel announces an even bigger edifice known as *The Sahara*. Grateful that we had at least been spared crossing that particular desert, we register for one night, dragging our infant paraphernalia up to a fifth floor room. Weary though I am, I can hardly wait to hit the gambling casino. A warm bath, a little lipstick, and I am ready for action. I nurse Jessie, burp her, change her, and quickly place her in the car bed. Karl trails dutifully behind me, sleeping baby in tow. No sooner do we step off the elevator than we are halted by a burly uniformed guard, his arm shooting across Karl's chest. "No one under 21 admitted into the casino." Did he imagine little Jessie wanted to gamble? A look of relief crosses my exhausted husband's face. He thrusts a ten-dollar bill into my hand. "I'll baby sit for awhile. Come on up when you're broke. Have fun." And he does a quick about-face into a waiting elevator. I am unchained! I am a grown up and I am alone in a gambling casino. I pause at the threshold of a miasma of sound and light, wishing to take it all in, unable take it all in.

I am twelve years old. I have been allowed to go downtown alone on the Illinois Central train for my Dramatic Art lesson for the very first time.

92

I climb the stairs and exit at the Van Buren Street station where sits the imposing Chicago Public Library with its lions on either side of its entrance. Beyond it lies the Chicago loop, all of it, including the Baldwin Building on Wabash Avenue, which I will cross by myself before entering this temple of drama and music. I have made this trip with my mother every single Saturday for six years, but now it has the feeling of a strange new world. Although I am expected home right after my lesson, I will bravely take myself to the Ontra Cafeteria across the street for a ladle of thick, delicious brown gravy inside a perfect mound of snowy white whipped potatoes. Always my mother and I would stop here for this favorite meal, after which I would go to the Ladies' room, and as I walked back to the table where my mother waited, I could pretend to be a grown up alone.

Now here I am, years later, hoping to appear a sophisticated habitué rather than an interloper. I take a few tentative steps across the carpeted floor. The noise in the cavernous room is a cacophony, the sound of heavy slot machine arms being pulled relentlessly, endless jangling of coins as they spew forth from their mouths. I have no idea what to do with the $10 bill clutched tightly in my nervous palm. Roulette, Blackjack, Craps, they are equally intimidating. I can bypass the big Wheel of Fortune, which looks far too simple and reminiscent of a Purim Carnival. I weave in and out until I pass a table where a seductive voice is calling out: "Place your bets, Ladies and Gentlemen." I stop and stand behind an elderly woman seated in front of a tall pile of chips. She shoves half of them onto a number just as the voice booms "No more bets." This must be a roulette table. The silver haired lady focuses on the spinning wheel. After the little ball comes to a rest, she quickly, doles out a number of her chips, slamming them down on the long runner in front of her marked "red." "Place your bets, Ladies and Gentlemen," the croupier's shout is a mixture of boredom and excitement. With his hand on the silver knob quickly comes the command "No more bets." I watch my lady shovel in what surely must be hundreds of dollars after each turn of the wheel. "Number 36" I seemed to hear over and over. I began to catch on. It didn't look too hard. Some of the numbers were black, others red. Some were even, others odd. A disgusted man suddenly relinquishes his seat. With all the bravado I can muster, I slip into it. "You want to play, Miss?" Sure. I hold up my bill, which is immediately stuffed into a slot and replaced with a pile of white, blue and red chips. I know by now that I can just bet on red or black or even or odd. Simple enough. I put one chip on even, another on odd. At the end of the spin, I have broken even. Next, with a show of confidence, I add one chip on red, another on black, breaking even again. This was fun. My $10.00 could hold out forever. But the next spin lands the little white marble on green or "0" sweeping away all my chips before I realized what was happening. Hey, nobody had explained "0" to me. It was getting late. Surely Karl must be itching to get down to the casino himself. I was nearly broke. "Place your bets." With my few remaining chips I decide to go for broke. I place one on black, one on even, and with unspeakable daring, another on the number "36." "No more bets." He spins. It seems to take forever before it stops. "Number 36, red." He looks in my direction and, with a slight smile, returns all my chips and counts out many stacks more. I have no idea how much money this represents, I only know I have gone from broke to rich with only one spin. A bosomy young woman in high heels and tight shorts appears magically at my side. "What would you like to drink, Honey?" I wonder how much the drinks cost, but with my new found riches I throw caution to the winds and request my favorite–bourbon and ginger ale. She returns with my drink, placing it in front of me just as red, even comes up. Lady Luck is still with me. "No charge, Honey." What fun! As I have seen my table mates do I take two chips from my pile and place them on her tray.

By the time I have downed a second drink my pile of chips has grown significantly, way more than I can attempt to calculate. The croupier is marveling at my luck, I am placing my bets faster and faster, wiser and wiser, when I see him remove his apron and step aside for a woman who quickly replaces him. "Place your bets, Ladies and Gentlemen" comes an unfamiliar, high-pitched voice. I go for red and even and 34 and 36. She spins and in what seems too soon I hear "15 Black" and my chips dwindle. Stubbornly I stick to the bet that has brought me such luck. Again, odd, and black come up. I glance at my Longines wristwatch that Karl's sister gave me as an engagement present. I seem to have lost all sense of time. To my amazement I realize I have been sitting at this table for nearly two hours! My poor baby! Karl will be furious. I must leave at once. Do I take my measly pile of chips up to room to pass on to Karl? But I am hooked. Just one more spin of the wheel and there is a chance that I could recoup all my losses and walk away with a bundle. Recklessly, I play number 36, but not so recklessly that I don't cover myself with a chip on odd. That way, I will at least have enough for one more spin. "00" Double zero, green," comes the nasal voice, and the entire table is swept clean. Double Zero? Green? A twin to plain "0" which I had ignored until now. I am penniless. There are no sympathetic nods or murmurings, least of all from the female croupier.

A pregnant belly, a full bladder, plus the fatigue of a long day make getting down from the high stool less than graceful. I fish in my purse for my room key as I make the long, dejected walk to the elevator. A carbonated burp erupts in the back of my throat. The confident grown up is replaced by a little girl afraid of what awaits her on the fifth floor. Not only had I stayed away much too long, I was returning empty handed. Will the elevator never come? When it finally arrives I am forced to share it with two jovial couples reveling in their good fortune. I listen outside our door before turning the key, anticipating a screaming baby and her floor-walking, angry father. Instead, I am granted a reprieve–greeted by the sound of my husband's snore and Jessica's sweet baby breathing. I fall into a sleep the moment my head touches the pillow, a red and black wheel spinning round and round faster and faster inside my head.

TWENTY-FIVE MILES FROM THE HEART OF BEVERLY HILLS

"Los Angeles, 153 miles." We leave Vegas. Soon its the dusty desert roads are exchanged for a maze of freeways. We push on, determined to reach Karl's Aunt Millie's before dark. Old Aunt Millie (who must be nearing seventy by now) has offered to put us up for the night so that we may get an early start in the morning to Compton, our final destination. I hope to navigate Karl straight to the Oxford Street address but when we reach the city limits the pages of the Thomas Guide, with their hundreds of street names in tiny letters, becomes harder and harder to decipher. Although Millie has warned us that their apartment is in an older, settled section of Los Angeles I am unprepared for the traffic, the stoplights, the tacky store fronts selling beer and cigarettes, offering to cash checks until pay day. Where are the palm trees, the bougainvillea, the Spanish tiled-rooftops? I cling to a notepad from last night's hotel room with scribbled directions from Cousin Judy. "Take Hollywood Blvd." she has emphasized, "until you make a left turn on Western Avenue." Here we are on Hollywood Blvd, in a neighborhood designated as *Silver Lake*. There is no sign of a lake, silver or otherwise, nor anything else to indicate that we have arrived in the City of Angels. "Stay on Hollywood Blvd." I caution Karl, who loudly assures me he is doing just that but suddenly; there is no more Hollywood Blvd. We are now on a street whose name is immediately recognizable to us both: "Sunset Blvd." Can this actually be *the* Sunset Blvd.? Where are the movie studios, the mansions? Something is terribly wrong. Karl finally relents and acquiesces to my pleas for him to telephone for help. He pulls into a Texaco Station with an open telephone booth in the

96

driveway. Dangling at its side is a chain holding a well-worn directory whose pages have been mostly ripped out. Fumbling for change, he deposits a dime for a connection. I hear him protest: "we *were* on Hollywood Blvd., but then it became Sunset Blvd." With a disgusted air, he puts down the receiver and walks a few steps to the corner to read the street signs. When he returns he insists: "That's right. We are at the corner of Sunset and Hollywood." Whoever is at the end of the line seems rightly perplexed. Years later we would discover that there is one point and one point only in Los Angeles where these two famed streets intersect. Either bad luck or bad navigation skills or a combination of both had led us to that very point.

We pull up at last in front of a five-story brown brick building near tracks that are disturbingly akin to those of Chicago. The apartment building itself might well be situated in the dingy neighborhood of Chicago's northwest side where Aunt Flo and Uncle Eddie had settled during the depression. My eye fastens on an old-fashioned fire escape running down from the rooftop and ending eight or ten feet above the littered sidewalk. I say a silent prayer that fire does not break out that night, leaving me dangling one story up as I clutch a babe in my arms. Who would choose to leave the Midwest only to settle in a neighborhood like this? Then I remembered the story: Aunt Millie did not "choose" to settle here, rather she was moved here in the late 1930's after a failed suicide pact with her younger brother, a dentist. "Doc," as he was known, succeeded in his desire for oblivion, whereas Millie had survived only to find a purpose in life by moving to California to care for her older sister and a spinster niece. Aunt Jean had succumbed to cancer two years earlier and it was for her that we had named our first child. Now Millie found herself the chief cook and housekeeper of Jean's daughter, Cousin Judy, and her elderly father, a retired painter at Hollywood studios. Uncle Sam, all 5'1" 120 pounds of him, had taken up permanent residence in an easy chair near a window from which he could inhale the odors of Aunt Millie's perpetual baking while listening to the radio and puffing on a pipe. The chair being near a window was irrelevant, for this trio seemed to have made a silent pact to treat windows just as any other wall, i.e. they were to remain shut and covered with heavy drapes no matter the weather. The oppressive heat was relieved only by the noisy *whirr* of an ancient electric fan, which seemed to suit everyone fine. The atmosphere brought to mind a Lillian Hellman stage set. It was into this cheery apartment that we lugged the portable crib up flights of stairs, and settled down for a supper of Aunt Millie's special pork roast. (It was believed that Millie had never married because she never found a suitor of her generation who not only spoke without a European accent but scoffed at the idea of keeping kosher). Dinner is served on china with pink rosebuds running around a rim of worn gold. I compliment Millie and Judy on the pretty pattern while thinking longingly of the carton of unbreakable brightly colored melmac dishes in the trunk of the Chevy, waiting to be unpacked. My usual insomnia took a vacation. By the end of the evening I closed my eyes on a rock solid pillow, dreaming at once of the beautiful suburb to which we would be moving the following morning.

COMPTON –
THE BEAUTIFUL SUBURB

A rainstorm during the night had washed away some of yesterday's humidity, leaving us with sunny skies as we drove south on what was later to become the Harbor Freeway. The freeway skirted bedroom communities with names such as Commerce, Norwalk, Downey, and finally, closer to our destination, a community called Watts. As we approached Watts our hunger pangs were severe enough to pull over and look for a place for an early lunch. As usual, I envisioned a charming place, a lovely place, a cool place where we could linger over a chicken salad sandwich on whole wheat. Instead we ate on a picnic table with peeling paint, in bright sun that seemed obscured a bit by a layer of brownish-gray. Could this possibly be that stuff in the air about which we had been warned—that thing known as "smog?" In lieu of chicken salad Karl brought me a paper plate of spicy chicken wings with a side of macaroni and cheese. My stomach protested but I had to admit that not since my high school days on the far South Side of Chicago had I tasted such mouth-watering food!

Our appointment with Dr. Cresswell Burns was set for 2 p.m. in his office at the Compton Sanitarium on Compton Blvd. The hospital ran for a stretch of several blocks along this street which was wide enough for four lanes of traffic, both sides lined with amazingly tall erect palm trees. The grounds themselves boasted beautiful lawns, shrubbery, and succulents. Patients were housed in white stucco bungalows with shutters at the windows and the red tile roofs for which I had hungered. I toured the lawns with Jessica in her little collapsible stroller while Karl met with his future boss. The sanitarium was a haven where I felt

I would be content to spend the next year of my life. I could make out the outline of a mountain range not too far away, bringing to mind my fantasy of spending my life as a doctor's wife at a Swiss Tuberculosis Sanitarium. Perhaps there was a cottage right on the grounds that a young psychiatric resident and his family could call home.

No such invitation was forthcoming. Dr. Burns and his wife Dr. Helen smiled graciously, bid us welcome, and wished us well in finding housing nearby. Should our search seem unrewarding, they suggested we begin close by, fanning out to other areas farther away. Once again, we were faced with a hunt for nearby affordable housing, only this time we had an infant in tow and another obviously on the way, and this time there had been no Cynthia to call ahead to a Mr. deLyra. For this I was grateful. We had the city of Compton at our feet. We were free. Perhaps we would even happen on a cozy little affordable house with a backyard where our baby could swing from a tree.

*   *   *

The best way to find housing in Compton was merely to slowly drive up and down the residential streets. Compton Blvd., with its tall palms on both sides was an anomaly. The farther away we drove, the drearier the terrain. Hand written signs announcing vacancies were propped up on a number of front lawns. Pencil in hand, I jotted down the phone numbers of those that appeared to be possibilities, for all too often, at the bottom of the cardboard was scrawled the words: *No Pets, No Children, No Negros.* The year was 1952. I cringed; surely Southern California was not the deep south. Was it too late to implore Karl to turn back, undo the past two years, to resettle in cosmopolitan Chicago and work with my *Stage for Action* company?

We settled for a boxy, charmless, grey stucco, non-restricted first-floor-rear two-bedroom apartment a few blocks from the Sanitarium. The windows looked out on a cement driveway on one side and a pathetic back yard in the rear. Electric dryers had not yet found their way to Compton. Criss-crossed clothes lines decorated the small patch of grass. Attached to them by wooden clothes pins were sheets and pajamas billowing in the breeze at all hours of the day. More and more I became aware of that brownish haze that seemed to hang over the air, obscuring what I had hoped would be the cheery sunlight of California. We awaited the arrival of our furniture in the large van marked "National Van Lines" that had last been seen carting our belongings down the elevator of our Brooklyn apartment. To tide us over we shopped for necessities such as a bed, a table, and a thrift shop easy chair. When the van finally unloaded our things I discovered a large rip in the fabric of the sofa my parents had contributed, plus several china wedding gifts smashed beyond repair. So much for the slogan of National Van Company: "From Our Door to Yours Without a Scratch."

*   *   *

As Karl became involved in his residency I struggled to adjust to what appeared to be my life for the immediate future. With another baby following so close on the heels of my first, there was no option but to give in. No need to scour the *help wanted* ads. I would not be leaving my house for a job anytime soon. Formulas and diapers would be my life. It's OK, I assured myself. I could wait it out. It's temporary. It won't be long before we will be able to afford a house on a bluff with an ocean view in an area known as Pacific Palisades. My husband might become a psychoanalyst by then and we would join others in a posh, interesting life punctuated by visits to exotic lands where he would present meaningful, ground-breaking papers. Meanwhile, I would content myself with life as a young mother. I could hardly wait for Jessica to walk so we could prance around in matching mother-daughter dresses.

While not as grueling as his internship, Karl's residency nonetheless offered him little rest. One night, in an effort to allow her perpetually sleep deprived father a few hours of extra rest, I had wheeled Jessica into the kitchen in her carriage where I rocked her to sleep. There she remained in peaceful slumber until I stumbled out to make a pot of coffee the next morning. As I turned on the water tap and glanced at her pink blanket my eye was arrested by a solid brown circular streak running its full length. Seconds later I realized that the streak was not solid at all, rather it seemed to be moving with a life of its own. It *was* moving! It wasn't a mere brown streak but rather an army of ants—live ants, moving slowly towards the chin of my precious baby girl. Scream, grab baby, plunge her into a bathtub! I had had to cope with the nasty stubborn little creatures during my brief stay in Miami Beach, and here they were again, stubbornly following me into what I had hoped to be permanent paradise.

The flies and mosquitoes of the midwest seemed mild by comparison, as did the few roaches we had encountered in Brooklyn. Daring to complain, I was chastised by Aunt Millie, who insisted that battling a constant army of ants was a small price to be paid in exchange for the perpetually beautiful California climate.

*   *   *

My belly grew bigger each day but whoever was inside was expected to remain there for another three months. Of the furniture undamaged in its cross-country move was a free standing torchier floor lamp. To soften the glare of an ugly overhead light fixture, we had placed it in the corner of our bedroom. On the night of July 26, 1952, I was awakened by that lamp swaying suddenly from one side to the other, bumping noisily into walls as it did so. The crashing sound of breaking glass brought Karl running from the other bedroom, where he had fallen asleep next to Jessica. "Earthquake! Earthquake!" with the authority of an expert. Cradling our baby in his arms, he pulled me up, and pushed me into hall doorway, which every good *Los Angelino* was expected to realize was the safest place. There we huddled on hands and knees for several moments until the earth seemed to relax. I clutched Jessica and stumbled into the living room easy chair while the ground reawakened and gifted us with several frightening aftershocks.

I was undone. The shifting beneath me had unsettled the foundation I had sought. Life would never be quite the same. I tried to settle Jessica into my breast but her usual sleepy contented feeling as she clung to my nipple turned instead to a restless whimper. The baby inside of me began kicking wildly. What was before a welcome experience as it announced its healthy presence, now seemed to portend danger. With every passing moment I anticipated an inevitable miscarriage, for surely no fetus could survive the rattles and shakes of what would later become known as the "Tehachapi Quake." Unfamiliar expressions such as *epicenter* and *Richter Scale* and *preparedness* would become part of my lexicon as I grew accustomed to the frequent jolts that were included in my dues for Southern California living, but now I wondered if it could be really worth it. An earthquake could spell the end of everything I had longed for. Though he was over a decade older than I, Karl would be impotent in the face of such danger. For the first time in my two-year marriage I felt vulnerable, alone. For the first time ever I experienced a pang of homesickness. Homesick for Chicago, the city I had rejected, had longed to leave. Seconds later I realized what it was. I didn't miss a city, I missed my father, my Daddy David. I was ten years old again, when Daddy had deserted us for his trip back to visit his father in Russia. My brother had become so ill he was taken to the hospital and our world fell apart until Daddy returned and made everything right again. My father could always make everything right, whether it was just because he cared about me so or because he was always ready to write a check. If he were here he would protect me against ants and quakes. I missed my Daddy. Our telephone still sat upright on the kitchen counter. Without thoughts of another aftershock nor of Karl chiding me for inflating our AT&T bill I walked the few steps, raised the mouthpiece, and listened for a dial tone.

"Hello, Daddy? There was an earthquake here tonight. I just wanted to let you know that we're all right. I just wanted to hear your voice."

**Down on the Farm with
Karl & Jay Landesman**

Mommy & Jess arrive in Compton

Jess & Aunt Millie, Los Angeles

**Visit with Uncle Ben & Aunt Gladys,
Beverly Hills**

PART FOUR:

SAN FERNANDO VALLEY

THE GREY FEDORA

We are in our first very own house! Acquiescing to Aunt Millie's orders, it is in the San Fernando Valley, but just barely. There are no freeways, so one of the only ways of getting to the Valley is via a winding narrow road which cuts through the Hollywood Hills called Laurel Canyon. Our house sits just over the hill, right on Laurel Canyon Blvd. on which pours a never-ending stream of traffic. The steady *whirr* of engines makes our front door practically useless, at least for holding conversation. Once again I have compromised. The house I wanted in the same development was one block behind ours, on a quiet street away from traffic, from danger to our little kids, but it was priced $2,000 higher. The real estate salesman convinced us ours was a real bargain so we had caved. (Had we not compromised, we would not have sold our house at a loss only a year later, but again, another story for another time.)

It is a sunny Saturday morning. Karl, in a rare mood, is planting a shrub with the help of his two little kids in the barren back yard. As a special treat I am going to make my speciality, egg salad, for lunch. All four of us love my egg salad. The pot is boiling and I am just about to plop in five eggs when our doorbell rings. Still wearing my ruffly cooking apron, I wipe my hands on a kitchen towel. Probably some neighbor children. Knowing I won't be able to hear voices I throw caution to the wind and quickly open the door wide. What have I done? No children, no neighbors, but two men in suits, ties, and grey fedora hats. Unusual garb for a Saturday morning, even in 1954. Behind them whiz one vehicle after another: snazzy convertibles, rusty pickup trucks, big blue Oldsmobiles. Not one driver would stop even if they could hear a scream coming from a Valley housewife.

Instantly my bowels are in an uproar. I squeeze to control them and press hard on the hand that grips the door nob.

"Yes?" In a voice much shakier than I intended.

The Suit on the left is a dark grey with a tiny pin stripe. Very classy. His deep red paisley patterned tie is perfectly knotted. In the button hole just to its left I catch sight of an oh-so-tiny American flag. The very sight of it causes my knees to shake. "Good morning, Ma'am. Is this the home of Dr. Karl Friedman?"

Who wants to know? I think, but I can only shake my head "yes."

"We'd like to speak to him. It will only take a few moments."

Suit on to his right is less composed. He wears an equally fashionable double breasted grey suit, but his tie is a bit askew, his collar a little wilted, as though the Valley heat has forced him to loosen it. No smiles.

These guys are not to be trifled with.

"Sure. I'll get him. Just wait out here." Shutting the door tightly behind me I cut through the kitchen to call Karl. On the way I untie the bow of my apron, tossing it on a chair. Walking as steadily and quickly as I can, I automatically reach to turn off the gas under a pot of boiling water. There might be no egg salad today.

"Karl. The front door …"

"You stay here in the yard with the kids." He doesn't protest; he doesn't ask questions. The look on his face tells me he knows exactly what this is all about.

As I keep an eye on my two munchkins I picture the scene in Compton, where just one year ago Karl and I were glued to our 14" black & white television screen watching Senator Joseph McCarthy destroy career after career, life after life. Many of the names were familiar to us, several were even friends. I squat on the brightly painted little child's step stool and soothe little Gilbert who has taken a tumble on the cement. As I gently blow on his "boo-boo" I wonder how I will be able to raise these two kids all by myself. Gil's elbow is bleeding and really in need of a washcloth and Bactine.

"Stay right here, Jessica honey, Mommy will be right back.`

I take Gil in my arms and decide to take him into the little bathroom just past our front door. I hear a low murmuring mixed with the traffic noises. Will the men see me? Will Karl be angry, thinking I am spying on him? After all, I am really not certain why they are here. Perhaps it is about one of his patients, having nothing to do with us. I could take Gil into the bathroom in the other end of the house, but curiosity propels me past the front door.

Karl's foot is in the door, leaving it half open. In his sweaty T shirt he looks tall and handsome. His head is cocked to one side. He seems unafraid but not belligerent. A wave of love sweeps over me. This is the guy I married, the one who is father to my children, the one I want to spend my life with. Behind him I catch sight of the two burly men who surely must be the FBI, who surely are here to question this doctor about his past, who surely are asking him to "name names." I must not linger or interrupt. I close the door to the little bathroom. I put a band-aid on Gilbert's cut. When I open the door again Karl has returned to the yard and is tending to Jessica. He gives me a strong signal that says "do not ask me anything, do not discuss this now!"

When the children are put to bed for a nap I ask him to tell me what the visit from the men in the grey fedoras was all about, but he will only answer: "Don't worry about it. They won't bother us again. I took care of it."

CHICKEN DINNER REDUX [*]

Throughout the 'fifties I was dedicated to being both a mother to my toddlers and a helpmate to my recently anointed M.D. husband. Being a good doctor's wife in the San Fernando Valley in those days meant getting heavily involved in the social life of similar couples. Like mine, most of the husbands were just starting out in private practice. Of paramount importance was the necessity of patient referrals from these colleagues. Only this would enable us to pay our mortgages and look forward to shelling out for bigger ones in the future. The result was a series of Saturday night dinner parties. It mattered not that few of us had anything in common other than fate having thrown us together at the same time and place. Our lack of real connection could be overcome after the first or second Manhattan or Whiskey Sour. Because there are a limited number of Saturdays in any given calendar, Karl and I were often booked for months in advance. Once invitations had been issued and accepted, we were inflexible. The date for a Saturday night dinner party was as difficult to change as a booking in Carnegie Hall.

It was our turn to host a dinner for twelve at our tract house in Van Nuys, where we had moved after our fiasco with a house on a busy boulevard. But there was a slight glitch. My aunt Flo and Uncle Eddie were scheduled for a brief visit on that very night. Flo wouldn't hear of my canceling, in fact, she insisted that she and Eddie join in the fun. This group was a far cry from their bunch of liberal pals in Chicago and I had more than a few trepidations. Not to worry, Flo insisted. She'd

---

[*] This story is reprinted from the author's first book, "You Can Take the Girl Out of Chicago." iUniverse, 2012

play the role of visiting aunt to the hilt and in addition would help serve and clean up.

By the time Flo and Eddie arrived early Saturday, my dinner was planned and prepared. We young wives had already begun the pattern of trying to outdo one another vis a vis the menu. (Later we would leave that to professional caterers.) With me, it was a question of making something very, very easy that looked very, very difficult. I had already mastered the art of the short cut, having discovered a marvelous barbecue sauce that was sold only at Love's restaurant on Ventura Blvd. If I was careful to dispose of the container, no one need ever know that I had not made the sauce from scratch. Freshly cut up chicken was laid out in a roasting pan, then covered and basted with this mouth-watering stuff before being popped into the 325 degree oven. Accompanying dish was brown rice with almonds—and *voila*! A tempting, sure fire, gourmet dinner.

Flo came into the kitchen to inspect. "This is it? This all you're serving? Don't they have a choice? What if they don't like chicken?"

"Don't be silly, everybody likes chicken!" I cried out with pre-vegan assurance.

My DNA was identical to Flo's in many respects, but her passion for "more not less" wasn't one of them. There we parted company, my mother's genes kicking in. "Just enough to go around" was my Mom's motto, whereas Flo's could best be summed up with "the more the merrier, the bigger the better."

Never in all her years of entertaining for hordes of family and friends had Flo seen such a Spartan array of party food. I had allocated one medium piece of chicken for each guest, plus just a few extra for those vultures who might want seconds. That would be plenty. The chicken had been purchased from Phil's, the very best fresh poultry store in the Valley. Money was still tight, there was no need to overdo, why clutter the refrigerator with leftovers? Of course, Flo and Eddie had unexpectedly arrived to eat with us, which cut down the number of extra pieces somewhat. Little did I worry, as I intended to serve plenty of chopped liver and onion cheese dip with the cocktails.

The little party was going off well, as anticipated. By the time we moved to the table at the far end of the living room (the "dining area" as it was then known) everyone was in a good mood. And ravenous. With Flo's help, we began filling plates in the kitchen. One healthy piece of chicken accompanied by a good-sized portion of brown rice. Green beans and salad were already on the table.

The chicken with the secret sauce was delicious–a huge hit. One by one, guests requested seconds. Flo and I went back and forth to the kitchen for refills. As the roasting pan emptied, a certain amount of panic set in. I glared at my husband when he, too, requested a second. Behind the closed swinging door to the kitchen, Flo and I exchanged silent prayers that the remaining thighs and breasts would hold out. There was really no backup plan–once they were gone, that was it! My husband would surely never get a referral out of *this* dinner party! Finally everyone seemed sated and we were down to one last drumstick. I walked through the swinging door and took my place at the foot of the table where I scooped up a few mouthfuls of the brown rice. The Manhattans had sustained me. Relieved that the crisis was over, that everything had managed to come out even, I could begin to enjoy myself. But at that moment, my darling aunt sashayed brazenly out of the kitchen, carrying a small platter heaped with rice and sauce and topped by one large drumstick. "Would anyone care for more?" she asked cheerfully, "there's plenty in the kitchen!" In anticipation of dessert, heads thankfully shook negative.

When the door had shut on the last of the guests and Flo and I began K.P. duty, we began to laugh. We laughed almost at hard as Flo and her sister Lily had laughed at Flo's rotund blind date many years before. And I laughed with the relief of knowing that once again, as with the flower petals at Flo's wedding, I had somehow managed to come out even. "There's more in the kitchen," I repeated to her, accusingly. But Flo was nonplused. "There *was* more" she insisted, "a lot more. I just never said more of what"

DR. GREENE AGAIN

In the years since my marriage I had had little contact with my Chicago analyst, Dr. Bernard Greene. I was aware that he had continued in private practice, a traditional Freudian Psychiatrist. As such, he had little to do with his patients after their discharge. I knew that "Bernie" (as I now referred to him privately) had assigned me to his "success" file, for after all, hadn't I fulfilled his expectations of marrying a Jewish doctor and giving birth to two children? He had scribbled a note of congratulations after receiving my two birth announcements, first a girl, followed by a boy a little over a year later. My latest change of address card had come from our house with a Van Nuys, California address. It came as a welcome surprise to receive a handwritten note telling me that he would be coming to Los Angeles and would like to visit me together with my husband, now a full-fledged colleague. He hoped I would be pleased that he would bring his wife Lee along. Flattery gave way to nervousness as the evening approached. Dr. and Mrs. Greene were to arrive for desert, by which time my children would be safely stowed in bed, assuring that our time together would be uninterrupted.

I liked Lee immediately. She was attractive (but not *too* attractive), warm, and open, as I had hoped his wife would be. Greene had put on a little weight, he had replaced his rimless glasses with flattering tortoise shells, but otherwise was the same down-to-earth guru I had known and revered. Over cake and coffee, he listened to Karl's accounts of his growing practice and the difficulties of getting patient referrals in a new city. He himself was longing for the day when retirement would afford him full time to play his beloved violin, perhaps with a good chamber quartet or even a symphony orchestra. While Lee and Karl were bonding I began clearing plates and bringing them to the kitchen sink. My analyst followed, explaining to the others that he would like a few private words with me. As I emptied the remnants of the bundt cake, he settled himself into a Formica kitchen chair. I had no idea what was coming, but instead of drying my hands and sitting next to him, I continued rinsing and scraping crumbs until he requested firmly that I give him full attention. When finally I took the chair opposite him, I was prepared for strokes for settling in to what must appear to be such a contented, fulfilling life. I certainly never expected what came next.

"You know, Dee, the world has changed quite a bit in the past few years and so has the field of psychiatry. Many of those old rigid rules have gone by the wayside. That's one reason I felt it was O.K. now to visit you with your husband in your home." I waited. Would he ask me if I was happy? Instead, he continued.

"Everything is a matter of timing, isn't it? During your analysis I was still locked into the old mores and traditions. I thought a woman could only be fulfilled as a mother and a helpmate to a man. We were taught to believe that women should teach school or become a secretary until the right mate came along. All that's changed now. If you were to come into into my office now at age 22, I would give you different messages than I did eight years ago. I wanted to see you this evening partially because I wanted to apologize in person. When you came to me you were unhappy, not getting along with your parents, and feeling unfulfilled. Sure you hoped to find a man to validate you, but you were driven to become an actress, and frustrated with your lack of success. You pleaded with me to help you overcome your lack of self-confidence. You even asked for my help a few times when you had an audition."

"I remember that," I assured him. "I was forever striving to be cast, I wanted to succeed, but I also wanted so much to please my parents and I figured you were right–that the only way I could do that was to marry and have kids."

"Dee, I failed you. I dismissed your needs. I misread you. If you were in treatment today I would assure you that there was no need to rush to settle down with a husband, but to keep persevering to fulfill your dreams."

Now he tells me? I don't know whether to be pleased or angry. Little Gilbert has awakened, crying for attention from his nursery. Karl will be expecting me to attend to him. I know it is my job, not his.

"Excuse me, Dr. Greene. I have to go take care of my baby."

LOCAL STAR

Mother. Daddy. Surprise. We're engaged!

Oh, Jerry, I don't know what to feel.

Well, I do, Sara. I feel like kissing the mother of the bride!

I bow. Thunderous applause. A standing ovation. I bow again, take a sip of water, walk gracefully on my high heels from the podium back to my front row seat in the synagogue social hall.

I am performing for a San Fernando Valley chapter of Hadassah, the women's organization which works in support of Israel. It's a far cry from Broadway, but the closest thing I can come to it until my two kids are grown. For now, the adoration of these housewives, their enthusiastic applause, must suffice.

Before leaving for college I had spent many years in Chicago studying drama and the art of performing monologues. At the age of four I had earned my first paycheck of $5.00, from my mother's sisterhood for my rendition of "Daddy's Little Sweetheart." I still remembered the punch line: *Oh, if mother hadn't married Daddy, Daddy might have married me!* By age fifteen I had become proficient at adapting and performing full-length plays, shifting my gaze from side to side, convincingly replicating the voice and body language of each character. At my last Chicago performance, given in a downtown auditorium, I had moved the large audience to tears over the death of Elizabeth Barrett Browning with my rendition of "The Barretts of Wimpole Street." *Oh, Elizabeth, don't leave me.* I lowered my voice for the poet, Robert Browning. My voice broke at Elizabeth Browning's last words *Farewell, farewell, Robert, my Love.*

118

Although this form suited me, it had never brought the same satisfaction as working with other actors and developing a role over a long rehearsal period.

It was 1959. Jessica was eight and her brother, Gilbert, a mere fourteen months younger. Our desire for a house overlooking the ocean in Pacific Palisades had been overturned by Aunt Millie. She, who had fled any connection to a Jewish identity, suddenly developed a love for the Chosen People. When Karl finished his residency and was about to start a private practice, she discouraged us from the long drive down Sunset Blvd. to the lovely Pacific Palisades. "There are no Jews there! You won't get any patients." She advised that we begin our new life on the other side of the mountain in the San Fernando Valley. Synagogues were quickly popping up over the hill; their membership rosters already included a number of young doctors starting out in practice. After due diligence, Karl discovered that Beverly Hills (close to the Palisades) was already overflowing with psychiatrists, whereas thus far the Valley boasted only one M.D. practicing this new specialty.

Our dream house on the bluff with an ocean view became instead a spanking new three-bedroom-two-bath with a thatched roof on Laurel Canyon Blvd. in Studio City. From there it was a quick trip into Hollywood, yet it was as great as the distance from Flatbush to Times Square. I attempted to adjust to life as a mother of two who would do everything in her power to help her husband become a successful doctor. Accordingly, I accepted an invitation to attend a meeting of ORT (Organization for Rehabilitation Through Training), a serious organization, unlike some others where fundraising was merely an excuse for a new dress. Reluctantly I tagged along to a meeting at the snazzy Sportsman's Lodge, where members ate a luncheon of rubber chicken followed by a talk by a celebrity. In this instance the guest was the beloved star of a popular television series wherein she portrayed the mother of a brood of boys. Though loud applause followed her introduction, I noticed the crowd's attention wavering as she droned on and on about her struggles to become a star, followed by a list of her many credits. By the end, the audience had dwindled to half it size. *And she's getting paid for this?* I thought, *I could do this, only better.*

Israel was just becoming a state. I was reading a book entitled, *Daughters from Afar* which consisted of first person interviews with several recent settlers of the brand new nation, all of them remarkable women of diverse backgrounds, each one more interesting than the one before. I set about editing the words of several of them, from a teenaged *kibbutznik* to an amazing concentration camp survivor. I perfected each character, complete with appropriate dialect, until I was certain I had what promised to be an entertaining and informative one-hour show. Next I locked in my first booking offering to do it *pro bono* in exchange for the publicity I was certain would follow.

I was right. *Daughters from Afar* was an engaging show, an instant hit. Over fifty women had listened spellbound to this moving, inspiring, sometime humorous story. My homemade flyers were gone by the end of the performance, my phone rang constantly, my calendar began filing with commitments for luncheon meetings as far as a year in advance. I resisted the many requests to donate my talent free of charge for a worthy cause, insisting that all causes were worthy and, as a professional, I must be paid.

There was one caveat to this new career. I insisted my performance start no later than 1:30 p.m. so as to finish by 2:30. In this way, I could usually arrive at my kids' school before the 3 o'clock bell rang, so their mama could drive them home as usual. Only with this promise did I receive Karl's blessings. After all, this wasn't show business *per se*; I would not be neglecting my duties as a wife, mother, chef, chauffeur, nor would I be out late at night hobnobbing with the theatre crowd. The Dairy Queen contract remained intact.

GOODBYE MY FANCY

I had begun to doubt my talent, my worth as an actor. True, I was a huge success on the Woman's Club circuit. I could adapt an entire novel or play into a one-hour solo entertainment. I could move a large audience to laughter or to tears, but was that truly "acting?" Could I prove that I still had the stuff to embrace a character, to relate to others on stage?

Several times I had performed at luncheon meetings at the Valley Jewish Community Center on Riverside Drive in Studio City. At my last booking I noticed a casting call posted on their bulletin board. "Auditions for *Goodbye My Fancy* by Fay Kanin, directed by Stanley Waxman." I knew of Waxman's work as an actor and his excellent reputation as a stage director. I admired him greatly and knew, too, that his professional career had been train-wrecked by Joseph McCarthy and the Black List. Would I be up to an audition? Why not give it a try? I read the script and discussed it with Karl.

"I doubt if I'd be good enough to actually get cast, but if I was, would it be OK with you if I had to leave the kids with a sitter during some rehearsals?"

Relief washed over me as I received both permission and blessing.

"Sure, Honey. Sounds like fun. Go for it."

Goodbye My Fancy is set in a small eastern college peopled by stock characters such as an attractive middle-aged president and a secretary with a caustic sense of humor. The leading lady, a successful Congresswoman named Agatha Reed, returns as guest of honor for the weekend of her class reunion. The stunning blonde stage and screen actress Madeline Carroll had originated the role on Broadway. The part in the movie had been played (not too successfully) by iconic Joan Crawford. In my wildest imagination I never dreamed of even auditioning for a Madeline Carroll role, much less playing one. I read the script, determining to go after the role of Woody, the wisecracking secretary originated by Eve Arden.

After giving what I thought to be a pretty sharp read for the secretary, I was a little taken aback when the director asked me to read the lead role of Agatha, I had no trouble identifying with this cutting edge feminist and delivered what turned out to be a more than satisfactory audition. At the callbacks I realized that Stan had already cast the character of Woody with a gangly hook-nosed redhead with a ponytail – a middle aged Valley housewife who was adept at comedy. Compared to her I appeared as glamorous as Madeleine Carroll herself. Angie cracked me up with her read. Her timing was already spot on and our scenes together immediately sprang to life. For the role of the suave male love interest, an attractive actor-turned-engineer breezed through an audition with perfect pitch. Already I could feel sparks between us. So there it was: without any angst or drama, I was thrust into my first venture as a leading lady.

The initial table read brought back the excitement of attacking a role from the start, of knowing that eventually this would become a finished product. By the second rehearsal when Stan put us on our feet, disenchantment began to set in. The supporting cast all came from tiring day jobs or their own kitchens. Except for the three leads no one knew stage right from left, much less upstage from down. Moreover no one was certain they would be able to memorize their roles by opening night. *Oh, my God, so this is what is meant by community theatre!* What had I gotten myself into? To bring this off would require weeks or months of rehearsal, but due to the demands of their families and outside work, three short evenings a week was all they could manage. Even Karl was amenable to a schedule like this. On my rehearsal nights I made certain than a hot family meal was on the table as usual. Marketing and cooking left me precious little time to work on my character, but I must show my husband that acting in a play in no way short changed him or my children. He obliged me by promising not to schedule late clients on my rehearsal evenings, but often I found myself waiting for the sound of his car as I flew out the door, the odor of lamb chop grease still clinging to my fingernails. On the nights I returned from rehearsal bursting with enthusiasm over a new discovery, a new insight or a new line reading, I would be rewarded with an indulgent smile before his attention turned back to Johnny Carson.

On opening night The Valley doctor-couples turned out en masse. Karl could not help but be proud of me, I thought. My figure had never been better and I had broken the bank by purchasing my own wardrobe. Brooks Costumers could not have done better than my two dresses and a smart suit with appropriate high-heeled pumps. The cast turned to me for the final curtain call, which I took solo. With humility I spread my arms acknowledging these amateurs who had worked so hard to turn this into a night to remember. Stan Waxman jumped on stage, gave me a warm peck on the cheek, an usher handed me a bouquet of roses. One more bow, this time in the direction of my husband.

Over drinks at the *Casa Vega* in Sherman Oaks after the show, the doctors' wives complimented me on my performance, several of them adding that they had majored in drama in college or performed in high school but had since "given all that up." Their underlying message was not lost on me

Sunday morning after the close I am at the built in electric range preparing Karl's favorite breakfast–rye toast and two eggs sunny side up. I anticipate, hope for, one more rave on my performance. In the breakfast area he glances up from the Sunday Times, and tells me how happy he is now that things have returned to normal. Normal. I freeze on that word. Butter sizzles in the pan; one perfectly cracked egg already begins to harden. I am holding the second egg in my right hand about to tap it gingerly on the edge of the pan so as not to spoil its perfect sunny circle. I feel its delicate weight but don't trust myself to crack it. The back door, which opens into the garage, is just four or five steps behind the range. I wonder if the car keys are in the ignition. I could turn around and be out that door and far away before he finishes the main news. I will the urge to pass as I tap the egg against the side of the pan, but my touch is no longer light. The shell smashes into bits and pieces, shattering the perfect symmetry.

SEVEN YEAR ITCH

I know why I waited
Know why I've been blue,
Just to be with someone
Exactly like you

The lyric keeps running through my mind as I look across the room at my still-handsome husband. The same words we heard on our first date at a jazz club on Rush St. in Chicago, the night I knew for certain that I could spend the rest of my life with the guy in the bentwood chair next to me, tapping to the beat as he held my hand in his. It felt so right to allow my hand to remain in his. Letting him take the lead was good–safe.

Of the other men sipping coffee in the spacious sunken living room, there is no one I would rather be with–no one I can even imagine lying next to. Doctors and lawyers all, not one of them comes close to being on my wavelength. Not one of them other than Karl could find the humor in this ridiculous show being presented for our entertainment.

A few years have passed since this group has settled in the San Fernando Valley. Our clothes, the decor, the menu, assure us of the wisdom of our choice. A uniformed housekeeper is clearing the dinner dishes in the dining room of this large Encino home, recently built to the specifications of our host, already a leading West Valley orthopedic surgeon. We twelve guests have been asked to carry our coffee and desert from table to parlor. We are six couples, an even number, always an even number. Singles have no place here. Nearly every Saturday night Karl and I attend such dinner parties where the cast of characters barely changes. Rather than participating in lively or provocative discussion, we are to be treated this evening to a full hour of color slides taken by our hosts during their recent trip to the exotic Orient. Our enthusiastic hostess will act as narrator with her husband assisting only if she might mispronounce a name or confuse a location. I roll my eyes at Karl, hoping he will catch the meaning behind my look, "how soon can we get out of here and back to our bedroom in Tarzana?" I do not plead a headache or a sick child. Instead, I shall sweat out the rest of the evening, pretending to enjoy it, thus proving to Karl that I am a good sport and that our lives have once again returned to "normal,"

A large white screen has been set up in front of the fireplace. Our hosts dutifully seat themselves at the far end of the room behind the projector. "Places please" I mime to myself in my imagined role as stage manager. A brief introduction by the Orthopedist is followed by the dimming of the lights. Almost at once we are privy on screen to Mrs. Orthopedist decked out in travel suit and carry-on luggage as she waves good-bye on the tarmac before boarding the 1960's version of a jumbo jet. Without dropping her memorized, well-rehearsed script, now playing narrator, she begins droning about the plane trip, the hotel accommodations, the exotic food, and eventually about the incredible bargains at the flea markets. The show is running on its own steam. My role as stage manager is no longer needed and I am in danger of dozing off, until somewhere between Beijing and Shanghai, I realize that we are no longer an even dozen. One couple has gone missing. Trudy and Neil are in grave danger of not seeing their hosts' trek along the Great Wall of China. Trudy and Neil are married, but not to each other. Max and Gloria, their respective spouses, remain glued to the screen, seemingly oblivious of the fact that several moments ago Trudy and Neil had gone out to the backyard for a cigarette, coincidentally at the same time. The plot thickens. The trek through China suddenly acquires an air of mystery. Am I the only one who notices Trudy and Neil slink back to the theatre separately and sheepishly some time later? Could this be included in the "normal" that Karl was so eager to embrace?

I wasn't worried. My marriage was rock solid. Karl was over a decade older than I and had already sweated out one divorce. Friends and relatives were constantly observing that he was "just nuts" about me.

Even if he should be tempted to stray he was locked into the rigid code forbidding any *hanky panky* between psychiatrist and patient. It was understood, in fact it was written, that should a doctor practicing psychiatry cross this line, his license to practice would be immediately suspended. As for me, I had done all the experimenting I could handle by the time I settled down at the ripe age of twenty-four.

On the short ride home I decide to play with fire.

"Well, I guess Trudy and Neil are having little harmless fun. If Max and Gloria noticed, they didn't seem to care."

"Do, what are you talking about? Harmless fun? There's no such thing. Believe me, there is *no such thing*. One time, that's all it takes"

"Karl, don't be so rigid. Everybody's doing it. You've got to realize that nearly all of these were wartime marriages. Almost all the girls I've met out here were virgins when they got married. Most of them got pregnant right away and didn't have time for any experimenting. And most of the guys went into the service before they sowed any wild oats. It's just sex. That's not a real threat to a good marriage."

"Trust me, both the Webers and the Nathans will be divorced within a year."

"Oh, c'mon. Suppose I had just a little flirtation. It wouldn't mean anything. You'd never even have to know."

"Once, *just once*. That is all it would take. End of discussion."

I put my arm around him, assuring him I had not the slightest intention of ever straying. Wasn't I in love with my husband? Wasn't he exactly l the man I had waited for? And hadn't I done all the sexual experimenting I would ever need to do? After all, I had gotten that part of my life completely "out of my system."

UCLA

1964 found me in the same house in Tarzana with essentially the same life I had known for the past decade. True, I had achieved a high profile as a performer on the Women's Club circuit but this career seemed a dead end. O.K., if Karl insisted on my becoming a drama coach, I would do it right. I would need a graduate degree in Theatre Arts and a few courses in Education. "Why don't you try getting into grad school at UCLA?" My husband had more faith in me than I in myself. They'd never accept me. My B.A. degree was nearly two decades old, I had not graduated *cum laude*, and I would look like a den mother. What the heck? I'd give it a try. Transcripts made their way from the University of Wisconsin to the admissions office at UCLA. Surprise! I'm in. Four mornings a week I leave The Valley behind and drive over the hill to a beautiful somewhat forbidding, campus in Westwood.

Not only do I find my academic studies stimulating, I am again caught up in the excitement of acting on stage. Instead of working against me, my age helps me get the more mature roles of older sisters or young mothers. I also paint scenery, operate a light booth, learn to run sound, all the time working side by side with students not much older than my own kids. My fellow students are mainly undergrads nearly two decades younger than I. One of my most eager partners in hunting for props and mixing paint turns out to be none other than Johnny Rubenstein–the baby who was born eighteen years before on a night when I was Isaac Stern's date and part of a group that congratulated the renowned pianist Artur Rubenstein on the birth of a son. Johnny loved hearing that story.

I forego the boring classes in education to concentrate on writing a graduate thesis. My choice of topic, triggered by my years of working with *Stage for Action* in Chicago, is to trace the history of the *Worker's Laboratory Theatre*–a company that began in New York during the depth of the depression. I immerse myself in research, spend hours in the library pouring over microfilmed copies of *The Daily Worker*. I even travel to New York City to conduct personal interviews with surviving actors and writers of the historic group. The research is stimulating and I surprise myself with the extent of my enjoyment in writing the paper itself. I would have wished for more enthusiasm from Karl–after all, this was *his* era, but he remains strangely detached. Two years later, I am rewarded with a Masters Degree in Theatre Arts. But there are no college or high school teaching jobs waiting for me. Leaving the Los Angeles area for a rural town is not an option and the few positions on local campuses are as coveted as a lead in a television sitcom. It seems that actors with "name value" had the same idea. They are now qualified teachers who had first dibs on any openings. With a freshly printed Masters Degree in hand, I accept a part time job with the Jewish youth group Hillel, working on Junior college campuses throughout Los Angeles, a job that would eventually become a game changer in my life. But that's another story for another time.

HONG KONG

Ironically, we sell the Tarzana house and move to beautiful Westwood just as I am no longer commuting to UCLA. As an alumnus I am on the official university mailing list. From the travel club arrives an announcement of a twelve-day package tour to Hong Kong and Taiwan. The trip includes meals, five star hotels, and guided tours. The tab is so low it makes staying at home seem extravagant. With both kids away at college, not only am I free to go but I am certain that at this price Karl will join me.

"Hong Kong? No thanks, no way. I have no desire to revisit the Orient. I spent time there during the war, came home with dysentery. There's no place I'd rather not go, but Do, why don't you go without me?"

Wow. What a switch! My notoriously possessive husband not only giving me permission but actually urging me to leave him alone for nearly two weeks. This must mark the beginning of a new era. Betty Friedan's magic has finally wormed its way into the male consciousness. But won't he be lonely? He assures me it's OK. Go ahead, have a good time.

He drops me at Bradley terminal at LAX. Our hasty goodbye kiss is tinged with trepidation and melancholy. I even offer at the last minute to cancel plans. My anxiety is reinforced as the plane prepares for takeoff. The Jumbo Jet is carrying a full load of UCLA alumni and partners. A quick assessment tells me that I am the only woman traveling alone. In fact, there is only one other single person aboard, and he is my seat-mate. Leonard Day is about a decade younger than I, tall, dark, handsome and remote. So remote that he responds not at all to my small talk. This is going to be a mighty long flight and an even longer holiday. But after a brief refueling stop in Hawaii, Len has had a drink and a stretch and upon re-boarding he becomes a regular Chatty Kathy. He's single, is an administrator at the VA hospital, and is already a world traveler. By the time we reach Hong Kong it is clear that we are soul mates. He likes touring a city by himself, but enjoys companionship at dinner. This suits me fine. When we are checked into the Peninsula Hotel and realize we are on the same floor, we make a firm commitment to meet at our elevator every evening precisely at seven p.m. when we will take off for the restaurant of choice. Our tour has provided us with coupons good for nearly every first class dining establishment in the city. I leave the arrangements up to my soul mate, the world traveler. He does not disappoint; our meals are spectacular, each one a unique experience.

Several times during our week in Hong Kong Leonard joins me on the early morning guided tour bus, otherwise there is a *Do Not Disturb* sign on his door. He later explains that he has "made arrangements" with the bell hop so that he need not spend afternoons alone. I do not inquire as to the gender of his visitors. Our time together in the bus is non-stop hilarity. *Sotto voce* snide remarks as couples walk past are followed by outbursts of laughter. We note with smug satisfaction that one by one the number of couples diminishes. First wives, then husbands, are felled by attacks of *touristas* or colds or sprained wrists or even broken ankles. *Serves them right*, we figure, for not traveling solo. We are the only "singles" and thus we are invincible. By the time we spend our three nights in Thailand, the rest of the travelers assume we are married and wonder aloud at our compatibility. The heat, the food, the wear and tear, confine most of them to the hotel coffee shop or the sanctity of their air-conditioned rooms.

The twelve days are up and I am anxious return home to share my experiences with my husband. True, I had found my time as a single more fun and liberating than I expected, but I miss Karl and am more than ready to again become part of a "we." A sea of faces waits just beyond the fence as we pass through customs. Since the world traveler has scoffed at souvenirs, Len has nothing to declare so I cajole him into carrying my new jade necklace. I am loaded with a stunning evening jacket for myself and trinkets for Karl and the kids, my cousins, my neighbors, that put me over the allowable total.

I scan the crowd. There he is, as expected, but something is different. This is not the Karl I left. This is not the pasty Karl who shuns the sunshine. This is a Karl whose face glistens and glows with an unmistakable bronze tan. His hair is longer and flowing. I look twice to assure myself this is the man I left less than two weeks ago. A hurried hug before I ask how he got that tan. His answer is quick in coming. "A doctor friend has a little yacht and invited me to go fishing with him last weekend." That's it. That's as forthcoming as he intends to be. On the drive home he dismisses my curiosity. "Fishing? What doctor? Have I ever met him? Where did you go? Who else went along?"

"Not important. I'll drop you at home and then I have to go right back to the office. You can tell me all about Hong Kong this evening."

But that evening I am too jet lagged to talk. I am asleep before his key turns in the front door. In the morning he has already left by the time I have my coffee. Len calls to check in.* It's good to hear his familiar voice but right now I have had enough of being a "single." I am happy to return to being half of a pair. I make my way slowly to the bedroom and begin to straighten our bed even though I am already looking forward to another nap. Like a good housekeeper I begin by pounding and fluffing the down pillows–first his and then mine. As I turn mine over something catches my eye. Some thing. My eyes are playing tricks. I am too tired to be doing this now. I lift my pillow and slam it down quickly in a gesture that would suffocate any living thing. Slowly I raise a corner of the pillow, certain the thing will have disappeared, but when I raise it again, there it is. Still there. At last I pick it up, run my fingers across it, turn it over in my hand. I am not mistaken. It is real. It is a bobby pin–a lady's bobby pin and it was lying underneath my pillow. On a rare occasion I have used a bobby pin in my dark hair, always black or brown. This bobby pin is a glinty golden yellow–the choice only a blonde would make. My hand is trembling yet I cannot let go of this

* Leonard Day and I remained close friends for several years. In 1977 he went missing from his job with the V.A. while taking one of several road trips to Baja, California. In 1977 his body was recovered, his throat slashed.

little piece of incriminating metal. I carry it with me to the kitchen, to the bathroom, hoping in vain that some sorcerer's magic will restore it to its original color, or better still, simply make it vanish. I place it on the kitchen window sill where it remains in my line of vision all afternoon. Surely there is some simple explanation. He will explain it to me and the lump in my throat will go away as we laugh about it together. But the lump continues until six o'clock when I hear the door shut behind him and I go to greet him holding the bobby pin in my outstretched hand. Not accusing, merely showing.

"What's that, Do?"

"You tell me."

"Looks like a bobby pin. Where'd you find it?"

"In bed. On my side. Under the pillow."

"I guess it must have fallen out of Luticher's hair when she changed the linens."

Luticher had cleaned our house twice a month for seven years. Her skin was dark mocha, her hair jet black. I did not recall ever seeing her wear a bobby pin of any color, but there it was, the simple explanation I had been waiting for.

"That must be it."

"Sure, Hon, that must be it or else how could it have gotten there?

That year the actor Rod Steiger won the Academy Award for Best Performance by an Actor in a Leading Role, but I swear that if my Karl had been his competition, Steiger would surely have placed second.

"Once. Just once."

Restaurant in Venice, Italy

Love Scene, "Goodbye My Fancy,"
San Fernando Valley

Dorothy Sinclair (Local Star)
Performing in San Diego

UCLA – Senior Thesis Production,
Freud Playhouse

PART FIVE:

LOS ANGELES

PRETEND GRANDPARENTS

I spend as much time with Jessica's two beautiful little girls as my busy schedule will permit, for I work at what is in the acting profession often referred to as a real "job-job." Hair and nails done to perfection I arrive at my desk in carefully chosen wardrobe at precisely 9:45 a.m. five days a week. I am the administrative assistant to a brilliant, witty literary agent in what has for half a century been revered as the most prestigious and powerful theatrical agency in the world. I field phone calls, attend meetings, read and evaluate scripts, take lunch with a variety of fellow workers whom I now call friends.

I reserve a few hours each weekend for Zoe and Keeley, aware of my desire for them to carry fond memories of their maternal grandma all their lives. I bring gifts, sometimes picked up at random in the local pharmacy—paper dolls and scissors, coloring books and crayons—more often carefully chosen dresses or pajamas from the exclusive Beverly Hills shop near my office. The granddaughters represent a lovely finale to the first half of my life. They are growing up—they are four and five years old—old enough to sometimes talk about their "Papa Karl." Papa no longer has a lady. No, Papa lives all by himself in a place called The Valley.

If he lives by himself, I fantasize, *why shouldn't Papa live with me?* Then I remind myself of the luxurious life I am now able to lead—luxurious in its privacy, its freedom. I am beholden to no one, responsible to no one, free to pick and choose how, where and with whom I spend my time. No, I no longer feel the need to share my space with Grandpa Karl. Why then do I catch myself looking longingly at the mature couple across the restaurant gaily ordering dinner for the adorable, well-behaved children who sit between them? Attractive and well coiffed, he in a Brooks Bros. blazer and striped tie, she in casual Eileen Fisher, they might well have stepped out of a print job touting a Caribbean cruise. Smug and smiling, they calmly entertain the precious offsprings of their precious offsprings.

When Jessica and Tom ask me to baby-sit on an early Sunday evening I readily accept. Somehow the signals get crossed and Karl also arrives at their Culver City house. Though we have called a temporary truce since the divorce, our relationship is strained, uncomfortable. Why not turn this accidental circumstance into an opportunity for creating a new scenario? The blonde bobby pin has long been laid to rest, together with the ashes of the lady who wore it. The new script goes like this: When Papa dines with his granddaughters and his capable, well put-together ex-wife (me) he will realize at last the folly of his ways, eager to rekindle our old flame.

I make a reservation at a favorite local Italian place where the little girls love the pasta and special ice cream. I greet the jovial, plump, perfectly cast maitre-d with a gracious smile and a little joke. Papa puts Keeley in a booster seat. He is all business. The ringmaster has settled us into a round booth in the center of the restaurant where we are seen and can be seen by audiences surrounding us. The handsome man I married has not lost his looks although he is a little worse for wear. No matter. We will play proud, happy grandparents to the hilt. I am all smiles, but Karl retains his cranky demeanor, refusing to play his part. He is ill rehearsed. His wardrobe is all wrong. Instead of a navy blue blazer he has made his entrance in an inappropriate short-sleeved striped cotton shirt. Of course summers are sweltering in the San Fernando Valley, but this is Los Angeles at night. The summer shirt adds to a gnawing realization that things are out of sync.

Nor are the two little girls performing as intended. Instead of being thrilled to be with us alone, they are cranky, missing their parents. Zoe does not like her pasta, which she complains is not the right one. Karl beckons for the waiter, insisting that he exchange it. I do not recall him ever making such demands in the old days. By the time the special ice cream arrives it is clear that this show will have a short run. Papa can't understand why we like this place nor find this particular ice cream better than any other. He dampens the girls' enthusiasm by ordering cheesecake for himself. The stares we are getting from patrons at nearby tables are those of annoyance rather than admiration. I imagine an actual round of applause as we make our hurried exit to the parking lot. The grandparents appear mutually relieved that the curtain has fallen on this interminable evening.

As I strap Keeley into her car seat give her a kiss on her delicious little neck I am already planning my wardrobe for Monday, when an ambitious young agent is taking me to a proper lunch at the Beverly Wilshire Hotel.

BIG BIRTHDAY

On the last Sunday in April, I park my red Volvo in the open lot behind the retirement home–the one across the street from the movie studio that was once MGM. On a bench in front of the entrance a well put-together, slender blue-gray haired woman waits for her ride. When a Lexus pulls up, she waves gaily and walks on her cane to kiss her son-in-law. *Nice* I muse, *that her family is taking her out for the day.* What springs to mind is the thought that Karl has perhaps become her friend. Karl, too, is now a resident of what once upon a time was thought of as an "Old Folks Home" but now has been replaced by the euphemism "Retirement Living." The double doors swing open to reveal a wood paneled lobby decorated in pastel tones of mauve and gray. Every attempt has been made to camouflage the true purpose of this facility, so that at first glance it might be confused with a luxurious hotel. The sight of several walkers and even a wheel chair or two quickly dispels this first impression. Small wonder the peppy resident out front was so eager to escape to the company of family from the world outside.

I was in this place once before when I accompanied a friend to visit his sister, who was showing signs of dementia. Now I am here on an errand of mercy, for it is Karl's 90th birthday and I have offered to honor the occasion by sharing his birthday lunch in the communal dining hall. I assume he will be pleased and proud to show me off. I assume it will be an occasion for *Auld Lang Syne* when we can compare notes about the grandchildren, perhaps even indulge in a laugh or two, despite Karl's deteriorating health.

My mother's words of warning over half a century ago still ring in my ears: "Don't marry him, Dorothy. He'll be an old man when you're still young." Well, Mom, I'm not exactly young, but I'm still a working actress, and I haven't lost my figure and with the help of my hairdresser, I'm still a curly headed brunette. Living in a "Retirement Community" is for me unthinkable. The doors open with a light touch, set as they are for the disabled. Seated just beyond the entrance hall are two elderly men, each with canes dangling from their chairs. One slaps the other lightly on his back as they enjoy a laugh together. I am in time for the punch line as the skinnier of the two chortles: "I've been in love with the same woman for 39 years. If my wife ever finds out she'll kill me." It takes a few seconds to realize that the man who convulses with laughter is my ex-husband. I am struck by how he has aged since the evening a few short years ago when we attempted to play grandparents in an Italian Restaurant.

Jessica tells me that Karl has made a friend at his new home—a close friend by the name of Arnie, who was once a trial lawyer. Arnie appears to be the self-appointed Henny Youngman of the facility. Karl and Arnie "hang out" together. Now I see them gawking in unison at the sight of a buxom nurse scurrying past. Karl finally looks up and recognizes me, with a "Hi. You're just in time for lunch. Have any trouble parking?"

I assure him all is well and hesitate a beat or two anticipating an introduction, an introduction that doesn't materialize.

"Hello. You must be Arnie. So nice to meet you. I'm Karl's former wife, Dorothy."

Arnie mumbles what passes for a greeting. "Pull up a chair."

"Thanks. I'll get one." I sit stage left of these two codgers and make an attempt at conversation.

"Karl, who was that pretty woman I saw out front? She must live here—she was just waiting for her family. I saw two really cute little boys in the back seat."

Karl was puzzled. "Pretty woman? Who could that be? What was she wearing?"

"A red suit and gold earrings and lots of other gold jewelry. You must have seen her."

Arnie picks up his cue: "Red suit? She must mean Marian. Marian. What a dog!" He pokes Karl and again their camaraderie is evident by a shared chuckle.

"Yeah, a real dog" Karl turns to me. "She's one of the rich old ladies who lives here. They play bridge together." The word "bridge" is delivered in a voice filled with disdain. (An image pops into my head of the night Karl trumped my ace in one of his futile attempts to master the game).

I start to disagree with their opinion of Marian, but I am interrupted by Arnie again poking Karl.

"Hey, here she comes!"

I follow their sight lines as a wheel chair comes into view from the wings. In it, slumps a mass of white hair tilted to one side, more asleep than awake. Gamely pushing it is a slender, curvaceous straight-backed young Asian attendant with exotic black bangs and perfect make-up. She looks straight ahead, but the Sunshine Boys are determined to detain her.

"Nancy, Nancy, how's Mr. Sampson doing?"

"Just fine, Mr. Arnold. We go to dining room now."

Karl persists:

"Nancy, Hi, Nancy, you know it's my birthday today."

"Good, congratulations, Mr. Karl. I see you in dining room."

There is no need to delay further. The boys rise on their canes and Karl points me in the direction from which wafts the unmistakable odor of institution food. As we enter the room Arnie hurries off to his own table, oblivious to any birthday celebration that might lie in store for his buddy.

No sooner are we seated than Karl scours the room for Nancy.

"Nancy, aren't you going to come wish me a Happy Birthday?

The polite, beautiful Thai woman leaves her charge long enough to walk over to Karl and put a hand on his shoulder.

"Of course Karl. Happy Birthday. And who is this? This your daughter?"

"No, no. This is Dorothy. Hey, Nancy, you know how old I am today? Guess how old I am? I'm ninety today Nancy. I'm ninety years old."

"Wonderful. Congratulations, Mr. Karl."

"Are you surprised? You think I look it?"

"No, no Mr. Karl. You no look it. I think you much younger."

Karl beams as the Waldorf Salad arrives.

LAST CHANCE

I'm standing on a step stool reaching for seldom used coffee pots and platters. I'm schlepping folding chairs borrowed from my neighbors. I'm ironing linen napkins. I have stowed my dog at "Doggie Day Care." As I run a bath after first pouring in obscene amounts of my favorite bath oil I catch myself belting out an old song in my finest New Orleans dialect: *Ah know why I waited, Know why I've been blue, Just to be with someone, Exactly Like you.* To a casual observer it would appear that I am happy, and I *am* happy, because I'm doing one of the things I love to do most: I'm throwing a party! In a few hours my guests will arrive. Well in truth it isn't *exactly* a party.

Karl didn't make it to ninety-one. He died in hospital on the Halloween night following his ninetieth birthday lunch. Jessica had pleaded with his doctors to extend her Dad's life a few more days, a few more hours. He was ninety and failing, I wondered why she couldn't make peace with letting him go. That evening she squeezed his hand and felt him return that squeeze, but she would never forgive herself for going outside for a breath of air and allowing herself to be detained for just a few last precious moments by some costumed Trick or Treaters.

When our son Gilbert arrives from the East coast he immediately sets about arranging for a final celebration of his father's life. As I pour them strong coffee sister and brother settle themselves at my dining room table making plans. I marvel at their strength, their judgment, and most of all at the extent of the grief that they share in this loss. When did Karl, who had robbed them of so much in the last decades of his life, become so precious to them? Why and how were their memories so short? Karl who paid scant attention to the neediness of his kids during their troubled years in high school. Karl, who was too busy tending to a neurotic new wife to witness the birth of his first grandchild. Karl, who seemed to pour a never-ending font of devotion and money into his stepdaughters.

I listen to my children in silence, for clearly I am not included in this momentous discussion. I am not part of this; I have failed in my role as wife and somehow, by extension, as that of a mother as well. I am but a minor character in this drama. I am invisible. I am no longer a presence. "Damn it" I swear to myself, "I cannot permit this! For so long I have been denied my place as Doctor's Wife, now am I not allowed the role of Grieving Widow? I pour myself a cup of coffee from my favorite mug, plunk down a plate of Oreos and insinuate myself between my two kids. "God Damn It" I think again, "I brought you into this world together with the man you are grieving. Well, guess what? I'm grieving too, and I will not be shut out or brushed aside." I keep silent, fearing that if I do not I will regret the words that are likely to spill out. I take too large a gulp of coffee, scalding my tongue, and run to the kitchen sink for cold water, still careful not to disrupt their train of thought. By the time I bring my glass of ice water back to the table they have moved on to the problem of finding a suitable venue for the memorial. They are squabbling like two little kids. Gilbert is advocating for a Rabbi, but rejecting Jessica's suggestion of a hall in a synagogue on grounds that it smacks too much of organized religion. "Besides, it's too cold and impersonal. How about your house, Jess?"

"I would, but it's just too big a mess, and my living room is so small. Besides parking is impossible. Cousin Janet's house would be great, but it's way too far out on Sunset."

My anger reaches the boiling point as they toss out and reject other locations one by one. *Here I am! Look at me!* I raise my hand a wave it like a first grader eager to show off the correct answer. Actor that I am, I succeed in lightening my voice by raising it a full octave to disguise my fury:

"Why not have it here? You could have it here, at my place. I'd be glad to have it at my place." I gesture to my spacious living room, the one still displaying tasteful antiques accumulated during my life with their father. One last chance. Allow me this one last chance to show the world, to prove that I am still the most important one, the one he really, truly loved.

Brother and sister lock eyes for a moment before voicing their mutual concern that I will not be able to carry off this event with good grace.

Reluctantly I admitted to myself that their trepidations were not without merit. Karl's second wife (or third if you figure in his army bride of many moons ago) had long ago overdosed on prescription drugs. Shortly after her death Karl brought one more love of his life to share his home. She claimed to have been a medical doctor in her native Serbia–she worked as an attendant in a hospital where Karl was a staff doctor. She was a great comfort to him in what proved to be his miraculously short period of mourning. Snapshots scattered throughout his apartment revealed her to be a platinum blonde with a thick mane of hair no doubt styled with the aid of a good many bobby pins. Despite a promise to help him through his declining years she had absented herself from his bedside during the last months of his life. I was assured she would not be notified of the memorial.

"Honestly, this is the best place to have it. It's warm and comfortable and the price is right."

That did it. With a final promise to be on my best behavior, my children caved.

Next step was to procure a Rabbi. Though a devout atheist, Karl had nonetheless developed an affinity for Reconstructionist Jewry, which is considered the most liberal form of the religion. A visit to the renowned Rabbi Chiam's office where they outlined Karl's life and set a time and fee completed the arrangements.

Family and friends begin arriving and I find myself playing gracious hostess, as usual. Jessica's colleagues from her workplace mingle with Gil's old law school buddies while my cousins chat with Karl's nephews as though time had stood still since their last meeting years before. I make certain people are introduced to one another. Conspicuously absent were any of Karl's friends, possibly because he had so few, either dead or alive.

An old classmate from the University of Illinois Medical School appears with his wife, she who had once been my close friend and confidante. Often in the good old days in Tarzana I had lent her my sympathetic ear during her husband's philandering and their many "trial separations." I had telephoned them at their ocean front home. Now here they were as I requested, shaky and wrinkled, but ironically, still very much together. I couldn't help wondering. *They look so old and worn out. Are they happy? Is it a good thing that they came back and back and back for more?* Once inside, they separate, deliberately sitting at different ends of the room. The living room is finally packed, the murmuring of voices could be heard, yet my sixth sense detects an air of discomfort, as though something is out of kilter.

The rabbi is late. My daughter decides that now is the time to deliver the eulogy she has written for her father, the same father I had perceived to be so neglectful of her. She stands, silences the gathering and begins to speak in a quivering voice.

"Everybody has a father," she begins, "but not everybody is so lucky as to have a father who is also a friend."

There are only two of us in the room. There are no other sounds, no voices, no scraping of chairs, no coughs no sneezes. It is as if a soft spotlight has been switched on to shine only on Jessica. From the day she was born I thought her pretty, now she was positively radiant in her grief. What is that she is saying? That Karl was not only father and mentor, but friend as well? I must focus on her words as she describes the weekends "Papa" spent at her house in his last years:

With each word I see the man I married and looked up to and laughed with and cried with. I remember the secret "code" words we invented, shared by just the two of us. I picture him pouring over the crossword puzzle in the Sunday Times. I see him with his harmonica cupped in his hands, tucking his kids in bed. "Old McDonald Had a Farm, *ee-i-ee-i oh*. With a chick-chick here, a chick-chick there, everywhere a chick-chick. *ee-i-ee-i-oh*!' I remember his broad smile as he held one baby in each arm. I blink, refusing to allow in my most painful memory, catching sight of him at a restaurant smiling at a strange blonde as he feeds her a nibble from his own plate.

Then Jessie's closing words: "I was so lucky to have a father who was also a friend."

She sits, dabs her eyes with the soggy tissue that is by now rolled into a tiny ball. She is spent. Job well done.

Lights up. Show's over. I am jolted awake. I resume my place. Yes, I am back in the leading role for the moment, but in truth I realize that it rightly belongs to my daughter who was recipient of his final love. This was my last chance. Now it's over.

The rabbi makes his appearance with apologies for his tardiness. I am of no consequence. No need for me to even bother to rise and introduce myself. Gil leads him to the front of the fireplace where he dons his velvet yarmulke, intones a bit of a Hebrew prayer, then withdraws the skimpy notes from his breast pocket. "We are here today to celebrate the life of …"

I had seen this rabbi many times on the *bima*, where he was poised and self-assured. Now he was barely recognizable, his confidence evaporating. Known for his improvisational skill, he seems suddenly at a loss for words. He admits he has only a brief conversation with the children to guide him. What had they told him? That Karl was a champion of the poor and downtrodden, that he had fought in World War II, become a successful psychiatrist, was a loving father and devoted husband. With this last word came a smirk from one corner, followed by an audible "Is he kidding?" A chuckle rippled through the room, encouraging the good Rabbi to wrap it up. "Well, I never really knew him, but I'm certain those of you who did are eager to come forward and reminisce."

Gilbert jumped to his feet: "Thank you Rabbi, but I'm certain that if my Dad were here he would agree that now is the time to eat. Lunch from *Nate and Al's* is now being served. Enjoy." Gil slipped the Rabbi his check and the assembled gathering was free to swap Karl stories. As the pile of sandwiches dwindled, snatches of overheard conversation were mainly those of praise for the quality of the corned beef. As for Karl, like the Rabbi, nearly everyone agreed that they "never exactly knew him"

**Pretend Grandparents,
Culver City**

Grownup Keeley & Zoe

"A Baby In Each Arm"

Printed in the United States
By Bookmasters